TO MELT A GOLDEN CALF

An Evangelical Christian Case
for Same-Sex Relationships

PETER AELRED

Copyright © 2013 by Peter Aelred
All rights reserved.
ISBN: 978-1-490-42995-3

All Scripture quotations are taken from either the English Standard Version (ESV) or the New American Standard Bible (NASB). Used by permission. All rights reserved.

Printed in the United States of America.

I give thanks to my editors: Mary Poletti, Jennie Ikuta, Virginia Street and Aimee Miller, as well as Jordyn Pritchard for the cover design. A special thanks goes to my wife, whose encouragement and endless patience help to sustain me.

This book is dedicated to my gay, lesbian, bisexual, and straight college students—a community that sometimes loves Jesus and one another so genuinely that I am re-taught the reality of the Gospel by their example.

Contents

Chapter One
Following Jesus into Heresy 1

Chapter Two
Why the Church Should Reconsider 13

Chapter Three
Classic Bible Verses We Have Read Wrong 31

Chapter Four
Paul's Letter to the Romans in a Biblical Context 54

Chapter Five
Other Attempts to Condemn Same-Sex Relationships 64

Chapter Six
Making the Biblical Case for Same-Sex Relationships 79

Chapter Seven
Gay and Lesbian Christians and the Holy Spirit 99

Chapter Eight
Biblical Equality, Human Rights, and History 110

Chapter Nine
Our *Imago Dei* and a Moral Objection to the Gospel 130

Chapter Ten
Reformation for the Sake of the Gospel 139

Sources
.... 157

Chapter One

Following Jesus into Heresy

For the first 10 years since I accepted Jesus Christ as my Lord and Savior at the age of 13, I was certain that all expressions of homosexuality were sinful. In fact, that belief preceded my conversion, since I was raised in a household that generally affirmed Christian morality. The sinfulness of homosexual behavior, instilled in me by both my parents and my church, was anchored in a deep conviction about the authority of Scripture too.

And let's be honest. If you're anything close to an evangelical, born-again or otherwise orthodox Christian, you're probably already questioning my credentials. Not so much my degrees and accolades, though. I'm talking about the credentials of the heart and soul. Do I have a commitment to orthodox Christian theology? Do I love and preach the Gospel? Do I believe the Bible is the authoritative and inspired Word of God? That's what I imagine you really might be questioning.

At least, that's what I did.

I considered the Bible's position on homosexuality so clear that I considered any attempt to validate homosexuality as on attack on the integrity of Scripture itself.

Even in my years at college, a time of my life characterized by a rejection of organized Christianity and embracing a selfishly personalized spirituality, I loudly defended the belief that the "gay lifestyle" was morally wrong, individually harmful and culturally erosive. From writing numerous research papers and commentaries to monitoring a gay rights activist group on campus for the College Republicans, I truly believed I was fighting the good fight.

As God brought me back to the Christian community, and as I exchanged my fiery political idols for a heart for seeing people encounter the Gospel, I still saw a church's stance on homosexuality as the litmus test for orthodoxy. If a church was unwilling to preach openly against the sin of practicing homosexuality, their theology was certainly suspect. If a church allowed gays or lesbians to openly serve in the congregation, they were practically apostate. I stuck to my guns too. The first church that would consider offering me a job as a youth pastor acknowledged that a gay man was serving as an elder. I sent them a polite e-mail declining the position, explaining that I could not in good conscience work at a church that didn't adhere fully to the authority of Scripture.

Nor was it too difficult for me to deflect exegetical arguments supporting homosexuality from more liberal Christians. They were simply ignorant of or defiant against God's Word. In retrospect, the intellectual arrogance that I carried then embarrasses me now. I already knew the biblically correct interpretation, so I was never more interested in genuinely listening to the biblical merits of other interpretations than I was determined to prove how they were clearly misguided.

I had plenty of ammunition to reinforce my arguments—not only the regularly-quoted passages that seemed to clearly condemn any expression of homosexuality, but also ample "scientific" studies performed by "ex-gay" ministries claiming that changing one's sexual orientation was indeed possible with God.

I also resorted to various *ad hominem* arguments to bolster my confidence. It was all too easy to point to a wild gay pride parade as the logical end point to endorsing anything other than biblically structured heterosexuality. I instantly suspected any theologian or pastor claiming a biblical argument for same-sex relationships of being captured by anti-Gospel, anti-biblical "liberalism"—if they even believed in Jesus at all.

Perhaps worse still, I viewed any testimony by an openly gay or lesbian person who claimed to be Christian, as at least delusional, if not deeply maligned and contorted by their sinful lifestyle. Perhaps Satan was using them as wolves among sheep to undermine and harm the Church.

This is not to say I hated gay or lesbian people in the least bit. I was very much of the "hate the sin, love the sinner" mentality. I believed that healthy churches welcomed people struggling with homosexuality so that they could one day find healing and a redeemed sexuality through the Holy Spirit's transformative power. I simply could not accept any idea to the contrary, especially when affirmation of same-sex relationships was adopted first and most prominently by leaders from mainline denominations who seemed to have no fidelity to the Gospel (such as former Episcopalian Bishop Shelby Spong).

So hear me out when I say that I followed Jesus into this heresy. Check my credentials. I worship Jesus as the one and only way to God. I place myself under the authority of the Old and New Testaments. I adhere to the Apostles' Creed. I believe that Christians are to take up their cross, die to themselves, and pursue righteousness. To put it bluntly, if you're reading this as an evangelical, born-again Christian, I am not one of "them." I am one of you.

As impossible as it might be to believe, my desire to follow Jesus faithfully led me here. I confess though I did not follow enthusiastically. The price for changing my convictions, and then actually acting on those convictions in any meaningful way, would be costly. Many in my own Christian community—even those I considered friends in ministry—saw me as heretical, disinvited me from their churches, and aggressively called on others to do the same. As a missionary who relied on donations to sustain a ministry to college campuses, my reversal cost untold thousands of dollars in support. Honestly, had I been able to avoid changing my mind about homosexuality, my reputation and my future job prospects would have been much better off.

A Reluctant Reversal

So how, then, did I come to believe that same-sex relationships are not inherently sinful? Looking back, there was no defining moment, but rather an amalgamation of experiences and research that brought me to this conclusion. However, I do clearly recall the catalyst. I remember seeing the constant emotional injury to gays and lesbians caused by Christians. Christians like me. These experiences accumulated to a point where I could no longer blithely rationalize away the damage that was being done to these people, men and women lovingly created in the image of God.

That damage, contrasted against the teachings of Jesus, began to haunt my doctrine. Actually, it was partially from the lack of Jesus' teaching, which never mentioned homosexuality in all his discourses on sin. Knowing that Jesus lived in a culture where some expressions of homosexuality were prevalent, his silence on it became gradually deafening. Yet, more troubling, was how Jesus challenged established religious doctrines of his day. On questions where it was agreed that God had already spoken to His covenant people, Jesus was asking the same questions again and coming up with different answers.

Numerous times Jesus is accused of breaking the Sabbath—working on a day set aside for rest and prayer—by the religious leaders. This was not a matter of interpretation either. There were very clear instructions on what actions violated the Sabbath, and Jesus was intentionally violating them by healing people. When interrogated by the authorities to give a defense of his behavior, Jesus appeals to His divine authority, but He also appeals to a new measure of doctrinal truth. Jesus responds rhetorically in the Gospel of Mark 3:4, "Is it lawful on the Sabbath to do good or to do harm, to save life or to kill?" (ESV)

Believing your doctrine to be correct because you believe your holy scripture said it was correct is not good enough theology for the Son of God. Please don't miss this. According to Jesus, the consequences of true doctrine should be in the best interests (i.e. restorative and life-giving) of those that it pertains to. If a doctrine appears to be harming others, then that doctrine may very well be incorrect—regardless of any alleged Scriptural references supporting it. Jesus reinforces this by even emphatically defending the breaking of Sabbath law by his disciples because he "desires mercy, not sacrifice,"

(Matthew 12:7) and elaborates on this theological litmus test in in the Gospel of Matthew.

> So, every healthy tree bears good fruit, but the diseased tree bears bad fruit. A healthy tree cannot bear bad fruit, nor can a diseased tree bear good fruit. Every tree that does not bear good fruit is cut down and thrown into the fire. Thus you will recognize them by their fruits. (Matthew 7:17-20 ESV)

The "them" Jesus is referring to are false teachers, namely the Judean religious leaders that prided themselves on their sound and biblical doctrine. Yet, while the Pharisees and religious scribes have a bad reputation among Christians these days, this was hardly the case in Jesus' day. The Pharisees in the first century were the rough Jewish equivalent of evangelical Christians today. They were deeply passionate about God's Word, correct biblical interpretation, moral righteousness, and creating revival in Israel to reverse the decline of moral and spiritual decay brought on by pagan culture. Historically speaking, since their formation in 152 B.C., the Pharisees did largely succeed in calling the Jewish masses back to the one true God[1].

Yet their rigorous and systematic approach to orthodoxy was far from perfect. So far, in fact, that Jesus claims many of their doctrines, while appearing biblically sound, yielded "bad fruit." As an evangelical, this was a nauseating pill for me to swallow, but it was undeniably Jesus' metric for winnowing truth. Jesus says spiritual truth will always correspond to good fruit, that is, restorative and life-giving consequences in the lives of those who practice it. Jesus also calls this what is commonly referred to as "abundant life." In the Gospel of John 10:10, Jesus contrasts himself to false teachers and Satan when he says, "The thief comes only to steal and kill and destroy. I came that they may have life and have it abundantly." (ESV)

This is how Jesus' teachings haunted my doctrinal house of cards on homosexuality. I thought that I, and Christians like me, were honoring the non-inclusive doctrine against same-sex relationships with all the grace and love we were called to display as orthodox Christians. It should have yielded understanding, repentance, and desire for others to draw near to God. However, all I saw in the wake of my orthodoxy was harm and spiritual alienation. If what I believed was really true, where was the abundant life in it? Was this actually coherent with Saint Augustine's time-honored doctrine to interpret Scripture through the "Rule of Love?" I tried to ignore the mounting questions, because I quietly realized I didn't have any satisfying answers.

That's where the questions began, but I really have to give the Holy Spirit credit even here. I can now see, retrospectively, that my beliefs were so certain, it is difficult for me to imagine having that significant of a theological shift of my own volition. Even with what I count as the work of the Holy Spirit on my heart and mind, it still took me more than five years to change from someone certain that same-sex relationships were sinful to someone willing to stand up for the rights of gays and lesbians outside and inside the walls of the church.

I should also be clear that I understand these rights not to be limited simply to a political sense. A number of prominent evangelical Christians, including the highly influential Dr. Timothy Keller, have already acknowledged that allowing same-sex marriage and gay rights within legislation and the greater culture is compatible within a Christian libertarian framework[2]. One can be for allowing the legalization of same-sex marriage and still be against gays and lesbians serving, leading, or receiving the sacraments in our churches.

The rights I am referring to ultimately include the right of total inclusion within the church body propelled by a renewed realization of our equality in Christ. This is my definition of the "gay and lesbian inclusive Christian" position referenced throughout this book, which I will simply refer to as the "inclusive Christian" position. The "non-inclusive Christian" position will refer to any view short of that.

I have avoided the more common "LGBT-affirming" and "non-affirming" labels for two reasons. First, while I do support the rights and equality of transgender people, the issue of gender identity is different than that of sexual orientation. Such a conversation still needs to be had in the Church, but it will ask different questions and will intersect with different Scriptures. While much of this book may still be helpful for transgender people, I want to minimize the confusion for a Christian who might be exploring the compatibility of same-sex relationships and Christianity for the first time.

Second, the Bible speaks far more about the inclusion of people than it does the affirmation of people. In fact, some would say that because of human sin and rebellion against God, there's very little affirmation of people at all in the Bible! Inclusion, however, is key theme in some Jewish prophecies, the teachings of Jesus, the New Testament epistles, and the Book of Revelation. I want Scripture to have authority even over my labels for this conversation on sexual orientation.

What follows then is my personal Scriptural and evidentiary case, modeled loosely after my five-year transitional journey, for fully including openly same-sex couples in our communities and churches.

How to Melt a Golden Calf

I begin with the motivation for even reconsidering the non-inclusive teaching on homosexuality in the first place. In some ways that is the most foundational chapter. If one were to disagree with the rest of this book, but at least accept the motivating premise for wrestling with this issue, I would be satisfied.

Following that, I'll examine the most commonly cited Scriptures, which have been used to directly condemn expressions of homosexuality. Since many of those passages have been significantly undermined by modern scholarship, defenders of the non-inclusive position on homosexuality have shifted somewhat from these deductive arguments.

Unsurprisingly, there has been new emphasis on inductive arguments that are derived from Scripture and that are more safely controlled by a subjective interpretation, rather than a concrete Greek or Hebrew language analysis. Challenging those arguments is becoming equally important. Lastly, I felt it was necessary to very briefly negate the arguments some evangelicals have used that derive from personal experience or research.

Yet I've realized even effectively negating arguments against homosexuality is not enough to persuade many non-inclusive Christians. Though contemporary culture is clearly overcoming what some evolutionary biologists have labeled as evolutionary aversion to homosexuality[3], resistance to same-sex relationships has become a hallmark of evangelicalism. It is one of the pet doctrines of the evangelical Christian movement. But the coherency of our Christian theology is in jeopardy when we hold up any pet doctrine to the level of a golden calf.

For this reason, the latter half of this book will be to devoted to showing that in order to maintain our defense of this golden calf doctrine, we inadvertently sacrifice much more established and essential beliefs on its altar. Our historically orthodox understanding of moral redemption, the nature of sin, the fruit of the Spirit, the testimony of the Holy Spirit, biblical equality, our belief in the *imago Dei*—these all must be distorted or melted down to form this doctrine against homosexuality.

To recover our spiritual riches, I believe we must repent of our idolatry and melt this golden calf back down.

Bold visions aside, you will find this book neither exhaustive, nor excessively academic. It is intentionally brief and written for the common Christian. Yet I do hope you will find it sincere, intellectually honest, and entirely motivated by a love for the Gospel. Realizing as well that no one book or paper or testimony ever changed my mind, I expect nothing greater from my own contribution to this discussion. However, if you are a gay or lesbian person reading this, perhaps in this you will find some peace and hope. If you are a Christian who is on the fence about this question, perhaps this will push you off of it. And if you are as certain as I was about homosexuality, perhaps God will use this to at least persuade you that faithful Christians who believe in biblical authority can faithfully come to different conclusions about same-sex relationships.

Who knows? With God all things are possible.

Chapter Two

Why the Church Should Reconsider

Before we can have a new conversation on the morality of homosexuality and same-sex relationships, we first have to determine for ourselves whether there should be any pressing reason to take up the issue. In many minds, including my own, the non-inclusive doctrine saying any homosexual act in any context is always sinful has been a doctrine of tradition.

Far from being a negative term though, "traditional" rightly implies that the majority of Christians throughout much of Church history found no reason to question this doctrinal position. Traditional positions on a whole slew of issues exist within modern Christianity, and, with few exceptions, most of them go on entirely respected and unchallenged.

So in one sense, the questions surrounding homosexuality are "settled" doctrine for the Church that needs no revisiting. I certainly believed this once, and many Christians want to end the discussion there. But in another sense, it is an issue that has never been fully addressed by the majority of Christians, especially not in the expressions that the culture-at-large is rapidly embracing today.

Despite the traditional non-inclusive position, Christianity's teaching on homosexuality has never been comprehensive. Debate on it has never reached the levels that would have made the subsequent decision binding orthodoxy, to the extent that such orthodoxy can exist. The Christian majority's condemnation of homosexual acts and same-sex relationships has never risen to equivalency of the Church's teaching on say, the divinity of Christ or the Trinity. But, even when compared to the ethics of abortion, our earliest historical records of the Church reveal a Christianity far more unified and vocal against infanticide and abortion than against homosexuality[4]. Despite homosexual practices being very prevalent during the rise of Christianity, the Church's attention and energy were focused elsewhere[5].

In fact, historians now possess some historical evidence that same-sex relationships were tolerated in much of early Christendom[6], and even officially blessed by the Church in some places[7]. Nor is this evidence limited to historian John Boswell's controversial research revealing lifelong "brothering" and "sistering" civil unions in the Early Church. There are other emerging primary sources that lend credence to the suspicion that not of all the rank and file of the Church had gotten the anti-gay memo[8-9]. This indifference or occasional support continued all the way into the 12th century, before a rising tide of Inquisitional anti-Muslim, anti-Semitic, and anti-homosexual sentiment brutally swept through Christendom and the greater culture.

When Same-Sex Relationships Became a Sin

Although the anti-homosexual agenda took wing with the French theologian Peter Cantor agitating for a Church-wide crackdown on the growing number of same-sex relationships in the priesthood and monasteries[10], it wasn't until A.D. 1179 that an ecumenical church council was influenced enough by Cantor to require punishment for homosexual acts. This was followed by Thomas Aquinas' magisterial *Summae Theologiae* in 1273, which officially anchored the Catholic Church against homosexuality[11]. Considering the age of Christianity, though, this places the condemnation of homosexuality by the Church even closer to our day than it does to Jesus' day. Same-sex relationships are relatively new category of sin as defined by the institutional Church.

Now, this is not to say that the Early Church widely affirmed homosexuality. Unlike women's rights in the church, we have no records of a nascent "gay rights" movement within the first few hundred years of Christianity. Whereas women led churches and taught over men until they were gradually banned from leadership by increasingly power hungry and culturally-influenced Church councils[12], the idea of homosexuality as a sexual orientation didn't even exist yet. Homosexual acts were labeled as sinful by some early Christians[13], and a rarely enforced ban[14] on male homosexuality was passed by the Constantinian Christian emperor Theodiosus in the 5th century[15].

However, we also find condemnations of any sexual act that was not intended for procreation as something that was contrary to nature[16]. The reason being that a vague Biblical precedent against it existed in the Hebrew texts (Genesis 38:9), and non-procreative sex indirectly undermined an univocal emphasis on sex for reproduction to create large families. Additionally, the most common rejection of this view would have been demonstrated in cultic sex rituals to false gods—not exactly the best role models for non-procreative sex.

Simply put, Christian teaching on homosexuality in the ancient world and the medieval era, as well as other expressions of sexuality, were hardly uniform. The claim that Christianity has always condemned same-sex relationships uses far too broad of a brush. Apart from the issue of homosexuality, this type of theological overreach is unfortunately not uncommon. The institutional

Church has been criticized before for naively declaring the timelessness of some of their very time-bound doctrines. From the Rapture and creationism for Protestants to purgatory and veneration of the saints for Catholics, all too often institutional leaders have few qualms about claiming the earliest Christians also taught whatever their denominations currently teach. The doctrine that all expressions of homosexuality are sinful is just another example of such a time-bound belief.

The Reason to Reevaluate

Christianity's teaching on homosexuality is far more of a historically recent doctrine than the kind of confessional doctrines that created the theological lines between orthodox and heretical churches. Yet, this understanding need not be essential to continue our conversation. Even if one is still convinced that until recently, all Christians in all times believed all same-sex relationships were sinful, a reversal of this magnitude would not be without historic precedent.

In the sixteenth century, emerging astronomical data completely overturned the Catholic Church's consistent and biblically based teaching that the sun revolved around the earth. This, however, was not an isolated revision. That same century saw the Protestant Reformer, Jean Calvin, reject Christianity's consistent and biblically based teaching against usury. Did Calvin invalidate the theological legitimacy or legacy of his Christian predecessors? Hardly. He was merely responding to the reality that the emerging capitalist economy was changing the context of charging interest from predatory lending to a healthy feature of a free market[17]. Whether it was the Catholic Church or Protestant Reformers, simply encountering new data and a new experiential context were theologically sufficient reasons for humbly revising doctrine all Christians in all times had believed until that point in history.

Even so, revisiting a doctrine that has more or less been consistent since the 13th century requires more than just a whim. Typically, the impetus for such an examination comes from an attack on the doctrine, either from within Christianity or without. The need to reevaluate a traditional position almost always accompanies a need to bolster the arguments for it. A good apologist, the intellectual lawyer of Christianity, updates his or her arguments on major Christian beliefs as often as there are challenges to them.

It is in this vein some might say Christians have already revisited the contemporary questions surrounding homosexuality. In having updated their arguments the way you might update anti-virus software, some Christians see it fit to consider the case closed. I believe a deeper and more thoughtful reevaluation is called for here. However, I also realize with that call comes a greater requirement to demonstrate the need. To approach the issue of homosexuality and acknowledge that the traditional view may need to either be modified or reversed demands a

Why the Church Should Reconsider

pressing and biblical justification.

The fact that it has become culturally unfashionable to identify same-sex relationships as a sin does not warrant abandonment of the non-inclusive position, or even that we consider abandoning it. When I felt deeply convicted that homosexuality in all its expressions was sinful and harmful to the one practicing it, I was continually frustrated by liberal Christians who seemed so quick to jump the orthodox ship in order to fit in better with the liberal culture. To me, nothing about their abrupt doctrinal shift seemed to be driven by a holistic biblical imperative. The best they seemed able to muster up was some ambiguous references to God being a god of love, which inexplicably made all non-inclusive teachings against homosexuality null and void.

This is the approach I hope to avoid, and I hope you wish to avoid it as well. Conforming our interpretations of Scripture to our cultural views and our own preferences may be expedient and satisfying in the short term, but it always undermines our spiritual growth in the long term. The 20th-century Christian writer C.S. Lewis said, "If you look for truth, you may find comfort in the end; if you look for comfort you will not get either comfort or truth only soft soap and wishful thinking to begin, and in the end, despair."[18]

If we believe that Scripture is inspired by God, how we treat Scripture is indicative of how we view God. To make Scripture say what we wish it would say rather than what it actually says, ultimately reduces the One really speaking behind the words down to a false god of our fancy. Said more plainly, in doing so, we make God in our own image, rather than the image He reveals to us.

So what is the pressing biblical justification for revisiting the traditional non-inclusive teaching on homosexuality? The biblical justification emerges from the observation that the cultural rancor over homosexuality has reached unprecedented levels in human history. This, in turn, is hindering the effective proclamation of the Gospel in a way that hasn't existed until now. Though there have been numerous times when homosexual expressions were tolerated or affirmed, the cultural and political battle for social and civil integration of same-sex relationships has never existed until now. The movement for gay, lesbian, bisexual, and transgender rights is not a fad.

Gays and Lesbians and Evangelism

To use Christianity's traditional position on abortion as a reference point again, the LGBT rights movement shows no sign of becoming a hot-button "football" that gets kicked back and forth across American culture. Do not expect to see generations taking turns being slightly more "pro-same-sex marriage" or "pro-traditional marriage" only to watch the pendulum swing back a little bit in the next generation. Support for LGBT rights increases steadily at a rate of at least

1 percent per year, with the last few years showing accelerating support. By 2012, the majority of Americans supported same-sex marriage, a massive shift from the 31 percent of Americans who supported it in 2004[19]. Whether Christians support it or not, the gay rights movement will be just as enduring as women's rights or African-American rights.

That leads us into the next pressing reality. Gays and lesbians represent anywhere between 3 to 6 percent of a given population[20], which means that there are between nine and 18 million people within the United States alone with a same-sex orientation. According to the Barna Research Group, homosexuals are about half as likely to be Christian as heterosexuals[21]. Using Barna data and metrics, if approximately 45 percent of the American population is Christian, then it is a reasonable estimate that less than a quarter of the gay and lesbian population has a relationship with Jesus.

That disparity alone should be alarming. Somehow, Christians have failed to advance the Gospel to a group of people who are just as in need of the Good News of Jesus Christ as anyone else. The attempted suicide rate among people with same-sex orientations is up to eight times that of the general population, and those who are transgender suffer even greater physical and psychological persecution. How can we have allowed ourselves to watch this unfold before us?

If you're a Christian, let's be honest with ourselves

for a moment. While there may be gay and lesbian sub-cultures, we don't view the LGBT community as an unreached "people group," as if we failed to share the Gospel with them in the same sense that we struggle making Christian inroads in Saudi Arabia. There really isn't a cultural barrier that can excuse us. In fact, even with the frequent cultural and language challenges, Hispanic-Americans are only five percent less likely to be born-again or evangelical than the average American[22]. Gays and lesbians, on the other hand, know just as much about Christianity as any other randomly selected American would. Some, of course, know plenty about Christianity, which is why they're not Christian. Why does it seem that so many LGBT people are outside the reach of the Gospel?

Some of this can of course be attributed to Christians' poor response to people with same-sex orientations over the last few decades. Calling AIDS in the 1980s the "gay plague" wasn't the best way to win hearts for Jesus[23]. Parents disowning and cutting off relationships with openly gay children in the 1990s wasn't the best way to woo them back to Sunday morning church services. Even now, Christian politicians offering up gay marriage bans in the name of God every election doesn't exactly scream, "Christians are ambassadors of the Good News!"

Let's face it, on so many personal and cultural levels, most non-inclusive Christians have been anything but "good news" for gays, lesbians, bisexuals, or transgender people. To many people who identify as LGBT, or who sympathize with those who do, evangelicals have been nothing but a source of fear, exclusion, and vindictiveness.

Trading in Sin

Yet to believe that homosexuality is a sin doesn't mean one has to treat LGBT with all the unkindness many have come to expect. In the last decade, many non-inclusive Christians have improved vastly in their consistency in treating all sin the same. Numerous pastors, even very conservative ones, have told me that they don't believe homosexual sin is any worse than heterosexual sin. Yes, acting on a same-sex attraction may be sinful, but no more sinful than the straight guy in the pew next to you on Sunday morning acting on his lust for the woman he met on Saturday night. In some respects, this is a great step forward in making gays and lesbians feel much less alienated from our churches and the message of the Gospel. It's more egalitarian, at least from a non-inclusive Christian perspective.

While this message from the pulpit is obviously an improvement from the sermons that preached that unrepentant gays would go to hell, it still belies a fundamental misunderstanding of homosexuality by heterosexual pastors. To compare all expression of homosexuality to particular heterosexual sins ignores the implication of what is taught in Christian sexual ethics. We are not called as Christians to merely give up sin, but rather exchange it for the blessings of God. True, we should give up any sin because it offends a holy God, but in practice we almost always give up sin because we realize it's fundamentally unhealthy. We exchange the lesser because God is offering us something greater.

With regards to heterosexuality, we apply this understanding of sin and blessings when Christian teaching commands us to hold to standards of sexual purity outside of a marriage covenant. It can be argued, that while it may be difficult to give up experiencing certain expressions of our sexuality in a premarital context, we do so because we believe that our sexuality is expressed to its best potential within a marriage covenant. To live otherwise, however enjoyable it may be in the short term, would ultimately lead to experiencing a "lesser" life in the long term (e.g. decreased intimacy, emotional security, sexual satisfaction). If one comes to internalize this belief on some level, it becomes much easier to avoid the sin of sexual impurity. This is because one is motivated to exchange the lesser offer of sin for the greater offer of God.

But when pastors say they treat homosexual sin the same as heterosexual sin, they can only mean this in that the gravity or seriousness of the sin is the same. They can't, in any similar way that they teach about heterosexual sin, ask people with same-sex orientations to give up the lesser offer of sin for the greater offer of God. Currently, non-inclusive Christian teaching can only ask gays and lesbians to give up the sin; it offers no true exchange for their obedience in the form of marriage blessed by God and sanctioned by His

Why the Church Should Reconsider

Church. The non-inclusive teaching commands gays and lesbians to refrain from experiencing romantic intimacy and sexual expression completely. Not until marriage, but forever—because as it stands, even marriage itself is something they must give up.

Some apologists have argued that while the exchange may be hard to identify, a genuine exchange still exists in another form. People with these enduring same-sex attractions must give up the tempting sin of romantic intimacy, and ultimately marriage, with those of the same sex. In exchange, God (and perhaps Christian community) will step in as a sufficient companion to keep them company while they spend the rest of their life without a human companion.

This does have an air of esoteric spirituality to it, an offering of holy satisfaction for those who really want it enough. To be fair, this is not unheard of within Christian theology. God-as-lover testimonies have existed throughout the history of Christianity by those who practiced celibate lives. Yet, excluding the stories of hermits and mystic-minded nuns, there is scant evidence that God offers himself as an equivalent romantic exchange for celibacy.

Celibacy is certainly a neglected discipline in the Christian life today, but lifelong celibacy has always been considered a spiritual gifting and calling—not an inescapable sentence. Even for those heterosexual people who long for companionship but find themselves in a condition of celibacy, we can at least affirm that their longing and hope is good, Godly, and pure. We can offer no such similar consolation to those with same-sex orientations, for even that very longing would be fundamentally sinful.

So even if we believe that homosexual sin is no better or worse than heterosexual sin, let's not kid ourselves about the weight and difficulty of what we're asking of gays and lesbians by demanding celibacy. We are not asking them to give up a lesser sin for a greater joy. At best, we are asking them to give up a lesser sin for a greater hardship. Can God still provide comfort within hardship? Of course, God can always comfort us. But given the incredible burden that non-inclusive Christian teaching places on gays and lesbians in the name of holiness and orthodoxy, is it little wonder that most of those with unrelenting same-sex attractions view the Gospel so ambivalently?

For the Sake of the Gospel

That Jesus died as a substitutionary atonement for my sins is good news, but if that also requires someone to ultimately give up any real romance for the rest of his or her life, then that good news seems immediately mixed with an awful lot of bad news. Accepting the Gospel as the greatest message one could hear becomes a much taller emotional hurdle to clear.

Some might even call it a stumbling block.

Herein lies the reason that we must reassess,

beyond upgrading our apologetic defenses, Christianity's traditional non-inclusive teaching on homosexuality. If Christians are truly committed to seeing the Gospel advance in the lives of all people, then it should cause great concern when we realize that by teaching that all expressions of homosexuality are sinful, we are directly causing millions of gays and lesbians to not receive the Gospel. It may sound old-fashioned, but our overriding priority, as followers of Jesus, should always be the salvation of souls and the making of disciples.

If any doctrine outside of those essential to salvation itself keeps countless others from being saved, then our fidelity to the Gospel should cause us to examine that doctrine—no matter how right we may already feel about it.

Please note, though, what is not being said here. Just because a teaching of Christianity makes it harder for someone to accept the Gospel, does not merit that the teaching be removed for the sake of making a softer sell. Jesus himself said there are many of his teachings that will make it more difficult for people to choose to follow him. The Apostle Paul said that the Gospel message itself is an offense and foolishness to those who are perishing without Christ. So to acknowledge that the non-inclusive Christian teaching on homosexuality will keep most gays and lesbians (and many of their supportive friends and family) out of the Kingdom of God does not necessitate abandoning the teaching.

It does, however, out of evangelical convictions, necessitate that we be certain that the non-inclusive view is actually true. To hold fast to the belief that all same-sex relationships are sinful may just be another necessary stumbling block that a fallen world is unable to accept. However, we must make sure that we are not placing an unnecessary stumbling block to the Gospel where God, in fact, intended none to be.

If we have been wrong about teaching that all same-sex relationships are sinful, there will be consequences for the Kingdom of God. Particularly as even an ungodly secular culture increasingly challenges the non-inclusive teaching as itself being immoral and inhumane, Christians run the risk of committing one of the direst sins of which Jesus accuses the Pharisees and religious lawyers of doing. In chapter 11 of the Gospel of Luke, Jesus tells them,

> *"Woe to you lawyers also! For you load people with burdens hard to bear, and you yourselves do not touch the burdens with one of your fingers... Woe to you lawyers! For you have taken away the key of knowledge. You did not enter yourselves, and you hindered those who were entering." (ESV)*

Removing "the key of knowledge" from others is one of the worst sins that Jesus accuses the religious leaders of his day of committing. It also means that God's wrath weighs heavily on the Judean religious leaders (all that "Woe to you!" business) because they are directly to blame for hindering people in coming into relationship with

God—precisely the opposite of their stated mission!

Note as well that Jesus doesn't seem to give them a pass for sincerity, either. The religious elites of Jesus' day were as devout as they came. They were no slouches. Jesus points out earlier in Luke 11 that they even tithe from their spice rack, which also indicates they were probably suffering from some obsessive-compulsive disorder. But whatever their hypocrisies, Jesus did not dispute the zealousness with which they believed they were the best representation of God. Despite their certainty though on interpreting the law of God, Jesus claims they have completely missed the point of a number of God's laws. They are wrong in enough critical places that other people seeking a relationship with God are loaded "with burdens hard to bear." The cumulative effect of these burdens ultimately hinders them from coming to understand the saving knowledge of who God is.

If it turns out that same-sex relationships are not a sin, and that by our teaching we have so stridently placed such burdens on gays and lesbians that they are hindered from entering into the Kingdom of God, then we are committing the exact same sin that the religious elites committed in Jesus' day. And woe to us if that is indeed the case! What mercy we will need to beg God for.

Again, let me acknowledge that this argument relies on the "if" clause being realized, which I have not even begun to demonstrate. Yet, given what is at stake with this issue, it should be self-evident that even the most non-inclusive Christian should be willing to engage in a critical reassessment of the traditional teaching on homosexuality. If Jesus' commission and cautions are any indication, our commitment to the Gospel and our love for people demands it.

Chapter Three

Classic Bible Verses We Have Read Wrong

"How could so many pastors get it wrong?" I've often been asked by non-inclusive Christians when they hear the claim that we've misinterpreted the Bible about homosexuality. The gist behind this question is often an understandable assumption that if enough respected religious figures come down on one side of a given issue, then that must be the correct position to hold. It seems incredulous that the majority, or at least whatever one considers a relevant majority, could somehow be wrong. Yet I've found that even very intelligent and wise evangelical pastors rarely give the legitimacy of same-sex relationships much thoughtful evaluation. While it doesn't take a scholar to consider the research, it does take an even-handed and deliberate investigation–something that few pastors have the time or genuine willingness for.

So though we may find it hard to imagine our favorite spiritual leaders getting it wrong on this particular issue, it would be nothing new in the history of Christianity. As we will explore later, the majority of pastors, ministers, and priests all at different points in history "got it wrong" on incredibly important issues of which there is little or no debate among Christians today. How?

Cynically, we could say that they were blinded by their prejudice or that they calculated to come out as a minority theological voice on a contentious issue would be too costly for them. Charitably, we could say they simply made an honest theological mistake or they were just too busy ministering to their flock to concern themselves with reevaluating a particular doctrine. Regardless, human nature has not changed since the Fall, so all these explanations could equally and adequately account for why so many Christian leaders have been so reluctant to embrace any form of same-sex relationships.

With that larger perspective in mind, we should first address the major Scriptural condemnations of homosexuality that are typically cited when your average non-inclusive Christian is asked why same-sex relationships are a sin. In some ways though this is the least important part of our conversation. Not because Scripture isn't our final word on matters of doctrine. Let me unequivocally affirm that it is. However, anyone committed enough to a given doctrinal position will not be persuaded by even the most robust and competent reinterpretation of the applicable verses. The very best one can hope for is a Scriptural stalemate, not a checkmate.

Still, I know of nowhere else we should begin. Below are the historically central passages that must be addressed as we discuss the biblical ethics around homosexuality:

- **1 Timothy 1:9-10**
- **Leviticus 18:22 and 20:13**
- **Genesis 19:1-5**
- **1 Corinthians 6:9-10**
- **Romans 1:21-31**

Commonly referred to as the "clobber passages," they are supposed to be clear, cut-and-dry condemnations that should settle the issue immediately for any Bible-believing Christian. However, with the exception of the passage in Romans 1, once I knew the linguistic and cultural context, I found these clobber passages actually possessed very little persuasive punch.

1 Timothy 1:9-10

I want to begin with possibly the most cited of passages found in Paul's first letter to his mentee, Timothy. It was the one I lazily referenced the most when I believed same-sex relationships were sinful. In my opinion, this is not the strongest biblical argument against gays and lesbians, but since the word "homosexual" is right there on the page, it was the easiest to use as a reference point. I also start with this passage because the best evidence for gleaning its meaning can only be analyzed in light of the Levitical passages pertaining to homosexual acts, which we'll look at in conjunction with our verse in 1 Timothy.

> *But we know that the Law is good, if one uses it lawfully, realizing the fact that law is not made for a righteous person, but for those who are lawless and rebellious, for the ungodly and sinners, for the unholy and profane, for those who kill their fathers or mothers, for murderers and immoral men and homosexuals and kidnappers and liars and perjurers, and whatever else is contrary to sound teaching, according to the glorious gospel of the blessed God, with which I have been entrusted.*
> *– 1 Timothy 1:8-11 (NASB)*

Fundamentalist Christians (that is, the more extreme end of the non-inclusive Christian spectrum) have historically considered this passage, and as we'll see later in the letter to the Corinthians, a slam-dunk condemnation of homosexuality. Homosexuals are included in the same category as "immoral men," alongside bank robbers, alcoholics, con artists, murderers in general *and* murderers of their parents. This has also logically given rise to the notion that homosexuality isn't just a sin on par with a heterosexual sin, but a particularly grievous sin associated with the most wicked of people.

However, an examination of the actual Greek creates a good deal of uncertainty. The translation of the Greek word *arsenokoites* by Bible translators as "homosexual" doesn't appear until the 14th century, when the Wycliffe English version of the Bible interpreted it to mean "thei that don leccherie with men." This poorly spelled phrase eventually evolved into a more accurate description as "abusers of themselves with mankind," which theologians interpreted then to mean homosexuality. However, when comparing the use of *arsenokoites* in non-biblical New Testament-era Greek manuscripts, there is very little use of the word found in all of our retained Greek literature. In the few places where it is used, it is never in a homosexual context. For example, the Jewish Sybylline Oracle, dated around the third or fourth century AD, reads as translated by J.J. Collins in a section he titled *On Justice*:

> *(Never accept in your hand a gift which derives from unjust deeds.) Do not steal seeds. Whoever takes for himself is accursed (to generations of generations, to the scattering of life. Do not arsenokoitein, do not betray information, do not murder.) Give one who has labored his wage. Do not oppress a poor man. Take heed of your speech. Keep a secret matter in your heart. (Make provision for orphans and widows and those in need.) Do not be willing to act unjustly, and therefore do not give leave to one who is acting unjustly.*

Clearly *arsenokoitein*, in this usage, is connected wholly to an exploitive context, and perhaps without any sexual meaning at all. Even as we move into ancient religious sources, the exploitive context remains unchanged. The apocryphal Acts of John from the second century uses *arsenokoites* exclusively in a similar manner.

> *And let the murderer know that the punishment he has earned awaits him in double measure after he leaves this (world). So also the poisoner, sorcerer, robber, swindler, and arsenokoites, the thief, and all of this band.*

Its use is not limited to economic exploitation either. A meaning indicating homosexual rape appears in the second-century BC *Apology of Aristides* in chapters nine and 13, and in the third century *Refutatio Omnium Haeresium* of *Hippolytus* in chapter five. The *Apology* tells of Zeus's rape of the mortal boy Ganymede; in *Hippolytus*, a fallen male angel named Naas rapes Adam in the Garden. By AD 575, though, its usage finds yet another context. Joannes Jejunator, the Patriarch of Constantinople, uses it in a written guideline for confession about sexual sin. It's found within a section near incest, and it says, "In fact, many men even commit the sin of *arsenokoinotes* with their wives."[24]

So we have at least three distinct meanings for *arsenokoites* from pre- and post-Pauline sources, none of which uniquely targets homosexuality itself as a sin. This has led many non-inclusive biblical scholars to suggest that Paul likely coined the word himself. So if we're to be entirely honest, no one can be completely certain what Paul meant in this passage when he invents the phrase *arsenokoites*, since it had never been used before (or at least used so infrequently as to obscure its true context from the contemporary researcher).

That being said, we can offer up some explanations rooted in the historical context of Paul's day. Given that Paul had an ample array of words to sample from so as to describe homosexuality in a way his readers would clearly recognize, it is particularly intriguing that he practically invents this word. Citing words he didn't use, *Erastes* and *paiderasste* would have identified men practicing homosexuality, likely in the context of an older and younger partner. *Arrenomicia* and *lakkoproktoi* would have described anal sex. *Hetairistriai* is just one of many words that would have identified lesbians. In fact, there is a significant list of other words Paul could have used separately, or in conjunction, to condemn male and female homosexuality in a way that would have been abundantly clear to his audience. Instead, we are left with this ambiguous *arsenokoites*. Why does Paul do this?

The most common theory, embraced widely by non-inclusive theologians, is that Paul is compounding *arseno* and *koites,* which taken separately literally means "man" and "bed." Despite some linguistic challenges presented by other biblical scholars, I'm also inclined to accept this explanation. Yet, even if this is the position accepted by non-inclusive theologians[25], who are attempting to prove Paul was intending to condemn all homosexual acts as sinful, I don't see evidence of the former proving the latter.

If Paul did indeed compound *arseno* and *koites* together, he would be doing so with some Jewish context in mind. Paul was a first century Pharisee by training after all. As it turns out, Paul's translation of the Hebrew Scriptures in the Greek Septuagint (which had already been read by Jews everywhere for two centuries prior), uses these exact words in Leviticus 18:22 and 20:13. Paul, according to the non-inclusive Christian theory, seems to be constructing a parallel back to Leviticus, back to when the Hebrew people entered the Promised Land to become the nation of Israel. Therefore, to understand Paul in 1 Timothy, we must be aware of how Paul understood the Old Testament.

Leviticus 18:22 and 20:13

Leviticus is another of the five most cited passages that are used to prove all expressions of homosexuality are sinful. However, some people choose not to cite Leviticus because a number of other laws laid down in it are hard to defend today. Leviticus 11:13 tells us that eating shellfish is an abomination or detestable. Leviticus 18:19 forbids a husband to see his wife naked during menstruation with a penalty of exile commanded in Leviticus 20:18. Laws like the ones enumerated in Leviticus, which can seem downright silly today, have led some Christians to abandon citing Leviticus altogether when trying to discern a biblical perspective on homosexuality. They rely instead on the more recent and presumably more relevant passages in the New Testament.

Whether this is done out of discomfort with the awkward contemporary context of Leviticus or out of a desire to justify homosexuality, I think we do a disservice to the discussion if we leave out the very Scripture that informed the worldview of Paul and the early Church. It's certainly not a faithful application of 2 Timothy 3:16, where Paul declares that all Scripture is God-breathed and useful for teaching.

If Paul is really directly referencing Leviticus 18:22 when he creates the word *arsenokoites*, a Jewish understanding of Leviticus will illuminate what exactly Paul might have meant when he used it in 1 Timothy. So what does Leviticus 18:22 say exactly?

> *You shall not lie* **(koites)** *with a male* **(arseno)** *as one lies with a female; it is an abomination.* **(NASB)**

Case closed, right? Paul must be against same-sex relationships, then. Well, not really.

Approaching this passage, or any singular passage in the Bible for that matter, as if it were floating in midair is a terrible way to understand its meaning. It's called "proof texting," and it's a favorite tactic of pseudo-Christian cults and sects for proving their most bizarre prophecies and doctrines. We at least have to look at the texts surrounding Leviticus 18:22 to understand what it means.

> *You shall not give any of your offspring to offer them to Molech, nor shall you profane the name of your God; I am the Lord. You shall not lie with a male as one lies with a female; it is an abomination. Also you shall not have intercourse with any animal to be defiled with it, nor shall any woman stand before an animal to mate with it; it is a perversion.*
> *– Leviticus 18:21-23 (NASB)*

The line preceding verse 22 commands the Hebrews not sacrifice their children to the pagan god Molech. The line following verse 22 forbids women from having sex with animals. It should give us immediate pause that male homosexuality and female bestiality are named to the exclusion of female homosexuality and male bestiality. Leviticus is nothing if not exhaustive, so it would be particularly odd that if the Hebrew community understood homosexuality to be inherently disordered, they would then leave out forbidding expressions of female homosexuality.

A fair question arises whether, because of the degree of sexism that existed in that day, female homosexuality is not mentioned because a woman's sins were less worthy of mentioning. Contextually though, this is very unlikely given that Leviticus notes women engaging in bestiality in the following verse. Additionally, sins that include women continue to appear throughout Leviticus.

Moreover, if verse 22 was intended to be a law on normative human sexuality, it's in a very peculiar place. The list of rules pertaining to who isn't allowed to sleep with whom continues on from verses 6 through 20. Sacrificing children in verse 21 signals a clear shift in theme, which would seem to include verses 22 and 23. But if verse 22 isn't about condemning same-sex relationships, what is it condemning? Verses 24 through 30 shed a great deal of light on this question.

> *Do not defile yourselves by any of these things; for by all these the nations, which I am casting out before you have become defiled. For the land has become defiled, therefore I have brought its punishment upon it, so the land has spewed out its inhabitants. But as for you, you are to keep My statutes and My judgments and shall not do any of these abominations, neither the native, nor the alien who sojourns among you (for the men of the land who have been before you have done all these abominations, and the land has become defiled); so that the land will not spew you out, should you defile it, as it has spewed out the nation which has been before you. For whoever does any of these abominations, those persons who do so shall be cut off from among their people. Thus you are to keep My charge, that you do not practice any of the abominable customs which have been practiced before you, so as not to defile yourselves with them; I am the Lord your God.*
> *– Leviticus 18:24-30 (NASB)*

Much of Leviticus, with all its specificity, is written as a response to the depraved culture and religion of the Canaanites, the people the Hebrews are in the process of displacing. Even very theologically conservative historians believe that the prohibitions on child sacrifice, male homosexuality, and female bestiality are specifically referring to the most offensive cultic rituals of the Canaanites as they worshiped their false gods[26]. This also provides further potential explanation for why female homosexuality is not mentioned in the text. Reflecting an ancient worldview that attached inferiority to being sexually penetrated, male penetration by another male and female penetration by an animal would have been seen as the epitome of defilement[27-28]. Far from a comprehensive condemnation on monogamous same-sex relationships, our passage in Leviticus is more accurately understood as a strictly gender-based prohibition of homosexual acts used in fertility rites, religious orgies, and temple prostitution.

Understanding Leviticus in this way also reconciles an inconsistency with the other Jewish law book, Deuteronomy. Interpreted by conservative theologians as Moses' updating and explanation of Leviticus for a new generation that is about to enter the Promised Land, Deuteronomy includes extensive prohibitions regarding sexual behavior. It also poses a significant problem for those who believe Leviticus 18:22 is about normative sexual relationships. Deuteronomy maintains the rules on normative sexuality that one would expect, such as those against bestiality and incest, but it leaves out any condemnation that could even be construed as a prohibition against same-sex relationships. In fact, Deuteronomy 23:17-18 appears to be the appropriate parallel to Leviticus 18:22, commanding that,

> *"None of the daughters of Israel shall be a cult prostitute, and none of the sons of Israel shall be a cult prostitute. You shall not bring the fee of a prostitute or the wages of a dog into the house of the Lord your God in payment for any vow, for both of these are an abomination to the Lord your God." (ESV)*

When we allow Scripture to interpret Scripture, Deuteronomy provides confirmation that Leviticus 18:22 is condemning homosexual acts within the specific scope of cult prostitution. Leviticus, in similar fashion to many of the stories we read in Genesis, cannot be accurately interpreted outside of its polemical context.

Now, this is not to say Judaism embraced homosexuality on any level. Through a combination of cultural and theological reasons, Hebrew religious leaders expressed varying levels of disapproval over homosexual acts. Yet these broader condemnations of homosexuality came later in Jewish extra-biblical commentary. Since then, the majority of Jewish scholars and the majority of the Jewish faith have rescinded those extra-biblical condemnations of same-sex relationships and welcomed LGBT people unconditionally into the synagogue community.

Genesis 19:1-5

But what about Sodom and Gomorrah? Surely that clarifies the ambiguous condemnation found in Leviticus. God destroyed these two cities because of their homosexuality, right? Let's see what it says in Genesis 19:1-11:

> *The two angels came to Sodom in the evening, and Lot was sitting in the gate of Sodom. When Lot saw them, he rose to meet them and bowed himself with his face to the earth and said, "My lords, please turn aside to your servant's house and spend the night and wash your feet. Then you may rise up early and go on your way." They said, "No; we will spend the night in the town square." But he pressed them strongly; so they turned aside to him and entered his house. And he made them a feast and baked unleavened bread, and they ate. But before they lay down, the men of the city, the men of Sodom, both young and old, all the people to the last man, surrounded the house. And they called to Lot, "Where are the men who came to you tonight? Bring them out to us, that we may know them [sexually]." Lot went out to the men at the entrance, shut the door after him, and said, "I beg you, my brothers, do not act so wickedly. Behold, I have two daughters who have not known any man. Let me bring them out to you, and do to them as you please. Only do nothing to these men, for they have come under the shelter of my roof." But they said, "Stand back!" And they said, "This fellow came to sojourn, and he has become the judge! Now we will deal worse with you than with them." Then they pressed hard against the man Lot, and drew near to break the door down. But the men reached out their hands and brought Lot into the house with them and shut the door. And they struck with blindness the men who were at the entrance of the house, both small and great, so that they wore themselves out groping for the door.*
>
> *– Genesis 19:1-11 (ESV)*

The story of Sodom and Gomorrah is somewhat surprisingly one of the most cited passages for condemning same-sex relationships. Surprising, because for over a thousand years Jewish theologians never interpreted the passage that way (as we'll later discuss). Even when we read of this story by the time of the New Testament in Jude 1:7, the author implies it was the attempted rape of angels, or "strange flesh", that symbolized the twin cities' evil. Contrary to the revisionist view applied by the non-inclusive theologians, the "sin" for which these two cities were destroyed was not homosexuality, but inhospitality. Genesis 18 records the hospitality of Abraham and Sarah towards three angelic visitors, and Hebrew theologians noted the explicit contrast in the following story of Sodom and Gomorrah. The prophet Ezekiel makes it all the moreclear by declaring, "Behold, this was the guilt of your sister Sodom: she and her daughters had pride, excess of food, and prosperous ease, but did not aid the poor and needy." (Ezekiel 16:49 ESV)

Trying to gang-rape angelic guests is hardly a Martha Stewart-style welcome, especially in an ancient Semitic culture that vowed to protect visitors at any and all costs. The behavior of the men in Sodom and Gomorrah would have been even more offensive in that day than it would be to us today. It is also apparent from the text that this was not a gang of homosexuals trying to prey on Lot's guests, but actually an entire mob of otherwise heterosexual men and boys. The passage clearly records "all the people to the last man" came out to Lot's home. Reflecting a common (though not universal) ancient Mediterranean understanding that same-sex attraction was compatible *in addition to* a baseline opposite-sex attraction, the author of Genesis takes for granted that this is a heterosexual crowd desiring to engage in violent non-consensual homosexual acts[29],[30],[31].

So as much as we may focus on the homosexual aspect of this story and think, "Homosexuality is bad!," this simply was not the focal point of the original story tellers or audience. It would be no different than if the belligerent townsfolk had been heterosexual females wanting to rape the angels and we concluded that sex itself was evil. Or, to use an unrelated politically conservative argument, it's akin to calling for a ban on all guns after a mass murder. To the ancient Hebrew audience, homosexual relationships are not even being addressed here. Like the rape of Levite's concubine in Judges 19-20 by heterosexual men, this passage simply assumes the normalcy of brutality that existed in the ancient world.

That is, until Philo of Alexandria.

The Roots of Revisionism

Philo was a brilliant Jewish philosopher in the Egyptian city of Alexandria who lived from 20 B.C. to 50 A.D. No fan of the kinds of homosexuality flaunted by pagan cults and imported by the hedonistic Greeks, Philo was the first Jewish commentator to reinterpret the destruction of Sodom and Gomorrah as a judgment by God for homosexuality. Philo's new interpretation, widely embraced by much of a

Jewish diaspora under the cultural assault of its pagan rulers, led the Jewish historian Josephus in 96 C.E. to associate homosexual acts with *sodomy*. He wrote of Sodom and Gomorrah in his famous work *Antiquities*, saying "They hated strangers, and abused themselves with Sodomitical practices." Unsurprisingly, these writings supplanted the traditional commentary on Sodom and Gomorrah's sin of inhospitality and were subsequently passed on into the theology of the early Church.

It's not surprising that Philo's exegesis of the Sodom and Gomorrah was so driven by his opposition against homosexuality that he would overturn orthodox theology. Nor is it surprising that the early Church could inherit bad theology. As much as we may want to romanticize the early Church as theologically spotless, it doesn't even take the gospel writer Luke long to document church fights over serious heresy in the Book of Acts of the Apostles. Moreover, the early Church's widespread acceptance of slavery, while culturally understandable, reveals that the Church—counter-cultural in many respects—was still a product of the wider culture in which it found itself.

What is surprising, though, is that despite the trending interpretation of the Sodom and Gomorrah story, neither Philo nor the early Church returns to Leviticus to make the same kind of blanket case against homosexuality that they do with regard to Sodom and Gomorrah. Again, the reason why seems fairly obvious: The traditional biblical understanding of Leviticus 18 was not a declaration of normative sexuality.

It's evident then that same-sex relationships were not the primary or even secondary target of any texts in Leviticus or any other part of the Old Testament when it was created, and it is highly probable that Leviticus is what Paul is referring back to in 1 Timothy. Still, how can we be sure that Paul understood *arsenokoites* to be male homosexual cultic sex acts and not same-sex relationships? Here again Philo of Alexandria returns to our conversation.

Given how educated Paul was, it's very reasonable that Paul would have read Philo, or at least be generally familiar with his work. As it turns out, Philo possessed a special hatred for homosexuality. He went so far as to advocate for the suspension of legal due process, so that people who practiced it would be executed. This is made more shocking in light of his reputation as a progressive thinker for his day, but remember, this was not 21st-century gay marriage. Philo's cultural context of homosexuality was surprisingly not so different from the context of the Hebrews, who entered the Promised Land thousands of years prior. Here, Philo waxes on the influx of pagan homosexuality in his city.

> *And I imagine that the cause of this is that among many nations there are actually rewards given for intemperance and effeminacy. At all events one may see men-women (androgynes) continually strutting through the market place at midday, and leading the*

processions in festivals; and, impious men as they are, having received by lot the charge of the temple, and beginning the sacred and initiating rites, and concerned even in the holy mysteries of Ceres (a fertility goddess). And some of these persons have even carried their admiration of these delicate pleasures of youth so far that they have desired wholly to change their condition for that of women, and have castrated themselves and have clothed themselves in purple robes...

In this text, Philo describes Galli priests and other worshipers of the fertility goddess, a scene that would have been commonplace in any major city throughout the Greco-Roman world at the time. Philo links the cultic fertility worship in Alexandria to Leviticus 18:22.

But if there was a general indignation against those who venture to do such things, such as was felt by our lawgiver, and if such men were destroyed without any chance of escape as the common curse and pollution of their country, then many other persons would be warned and corrected by their example[32].

Brutality aside, this last line is critical to our discussion. The lawgiver here is Moses, to whom Jews (and Christians) attributed the laws of Leviticus. Philo, one of the most influential Jewish thinkers of Paul's day, believed Leviticus 18:22 was a prohibition on homosexual acts in cultic worship and orgies. This understanding of Leviticus also means *arseno* and *koites*, the Greek wording of Leviticus 18:22, had for Philo the same equivalency.

Therefore, it is hard to imagine a scenario where his Jewish contemporary Paul would fuse the two words together with a different definition from that of Philo while forgoing an explanation. To attempt so today on behalf of Paul would be not only linguistic folly, but also an abandonment of the authority of Scripture. Ironically, in their efforts to defend the non-inclusive doctrine against homosexuality, many Christians may inadvertently place themselves over the Scripture attempting to get Paul to say what they wish Paul would say.

1 Corinthians 6:9-10

In spite of a compelling argument that Paul was referring to temple cultic rituals in Timothy, some non-inclusive theologians believe that Paul's additional wording in 1 Corinthians 6:9-11 makes a better case against homosexuality.

> *Or do you not know that the unrighteous will not inherit the kingdom of God? Do not be deceived; neither fornicators, nor idolaters, nor adulterers, nor effeminate, nor homosexuals (abusers of themselves with mankind), nor thieves, nor the covetous, nor drunkards, nor revilers, nor swindlers, will inherit the kingdom of God. Such were some of you; but you were washed, but you were sanctified, but you were justified in the name of the Lord Jesus Christ and in the Spirit of our God. (NASB)*

Paul here again uses *arsenokoites* in a way that most translations interpret to mean homosexuals. The argument would be no different from our previous discussion except that non-inclusive theologians have jumped on the word preceding *arsenokoites*. The word, *malakos*, usually translated in contemporary Bibles as "effeminate," has recently been held up by some non-inclusive Christians as evidence that Paul was referencing both passive and active partners in a homosexual relationship, effectively creating a trickle down effect into some modern versions of the Bible[33].

This is something of an ad hoc argument, though, since for hundreds of years Christians, including the likes of Martin Luther and Jean Calvin, effectively translated the word to mean "weakling" without even the remotest connection to homosexuality. It was not until the 1600s that translators began to interpret *malakos* as effeminate in the newly minted King James Bible and not until the 1900s that any Bible identified the word with homosexuality[34].

A significant difference with *malakos* compared to *arsenokoites,* is that there is ample evidence of what it really means, literally "soft" as defined in Strong's Exhaustive Concordance. However, the deeper cultural meaning incorporates the sexist language of the ancient world that associated women with weakness, vanity, emotionalism, and uncontrolled passion. This diverse pejorative turned *malakos* into a word that was used to describe an entire range of behaviors. It is true that *malakos* was on some occasions in Greek writings, used to describe men who desired to be penetrated, though it seems as if this was almost entirely confined to men who were already engaging in heterosexual sex acts[35]. But *malakos* was most often used to describe those who were decadent, weak-willed, vain, and even very attractive boys. Even in a sexual context, the most frequent referrals are about men submitting to women. For example, in a play by Aristophanes, an old spinster carries off a young man, exclaiming, "Come along, my little softie" (*malakion*)[36].

So is Paul using *malakos* to mean a callboy, a playboy, or a decadent, vain person? We simply can't know, but since the words *pathikos* and *kinaidos* would have clearly indicated a passive homosexual partner, we can logically rule out that *malakos* would have been used for that particular meaning. Additionally, because Paul also doesn't place this word next to *arsenokoites* in 1 Timothy 1:8-11, it would be an incredible leap to say Paul could have ever intended these words to be corresponding passive and active male partners. But even if he did, consider what we conclusively know about *arsenokoites* referring to temple prostitution. At most, and it is quite a stretch to get even here, *malakos* could refer to male temple prostitutes and *arsenokoites* to the men that visit the temple for sexual services. At any rate, this can hardly be taken as blanket condemnation of same-sex relationships.

The Need for Cognitive Humility

Now, by this point, if you are skeptical that homosexuality could ever be permissible by God, you may have already looked up my arguments on the Internet for the appropriate non-inclusive Christian rebuttal. I know I would have. Particularly as we splice and dice the Greek and Hebrew meanings of words, it is all too easy to find some "scholar" on the web who will tell you just what your doctrine wants to hear. Yet I am not making cutting-edge or radical claims of scholarship, so you need not worry about outmatching my credentials. I am also aware that by this stage in my commitment to defending same-sex relationships, I too want the translations to affirm my position, and am less inclined to consider those translations that would not.

That confession being made, my request of you is not that you would be swayed so completely as to believe that these clobber passages have been misinterpreted and misappropriated. My request is simply that you would acknowledge that they are grayer than you previously might have thought. Possessing the cognitive humility about the possibility that other intelligent, sincere and Gospel-centered Christians *may* have unearthed a more accurate understanding of these texts is, I believe, a God-honoring approach that would not in any way sacrifice your current doctrinal convictions.

Chapter Four

Paul's Letter to the Romans in a Biblical Context

So far we've established the dubiousness, if not complete irrelevance, of the previous texts that non-inclusive Christians say prove homosexuality is, in all forms, sinful. Still, there is one verse in the Bible that is more immune to ideological manipulation. For non-inclusive Christians dedicated to proving that homosexuality is a dire sin, Romans 1:26-27 provides a proof text that is hard to get lost in translation.

> *For this reason God gave them up to dishonorable passions. For their women exchanged natural relations*

> *for those that are contrary to nature; and the men likewise gave up natural relations with women and were consumed with passion for one another, men committing shameless acts with men and receiving in themselves the due penalty for their error. (ESV)*

Unlike all of the previous passages we've examined, the difference of interpretation is not a matter of understanding the proper Greek or Hebrew. Paul is in no uncertain terms describing homosexual acts, rather than just potentially referring to them. On a personal note, this passage was for me the most difficult to reconcile with a pro-gay position when I first began reevaluating the issue. Unlike any other passage in the Bible, Paul describes not only male homosexuality, but also female homosexuality. Additionally, he seems to be making an argument that homosexuality is against "nature" itself.

Not wanting to delete this very prominent and articulated condemnation of homosexuality in order to have a more palatable Bible, I refused to let myself go any further in my questioning of the non-inclusive doctrine against same-sex relationships. I was on the theological fence for years over these verses in Romans 1, that is, until someone told me to read the *entire* narrative in Romans 1.

> *For the wrath of God is revealed from heaven against all ungodliness and unrighteousness of men, who by their unrighteousness suppress the truth. For what can be known about God is plain to them, because God has shown it to them. For his invisible attributes, namely,*

his eternal power and divine nature, have been clearly perceived, ever since the creation of the world, in the things that have been made. So they are without excuse. For although they knew God, they did not honor him as God or give thanks to him, but they became futile in their thinking, and their foolish hearts were darkened. Claiming to be wise, they became fools, and exchanged the glory of the immortal God for images resembling mortal man and birds and animals and creeping things.

Therefore God gave them up in the lusts of their hearts to impurity, to the dishonoring of their bodies among themselves, because they exchanged the truth about God for a lie and worshiped and served the creature rather than the Creator, who is blessed forever! Amen.

For this reason God gave them up to dishonorable passions. For their women exchanged natural relations for those that are contrary to nature; and the men likewise gave up natural relations with women and were consumed with passion for one another, men committing shameless acts with men and receiving in themselves the due penalty for their error.

And since they did not see fit to acknowledge God, God gave them up to a debased mind to do what ought not to be done. They were filled with all manner of unrighteousness, evil, covetousness, malice. They are full of envy, murder, strife, deceit and maliciousness. They are gossips, slanderers, haters of God, insolent, haughty, boastful, inventors of evil, disobedient to parents, foolish, faithless, heartless, ruthless. Though they know God's righteous decree that those who practice such things deserve to die, they not only do them, but give approval to those who practice them. (ESV)

Unwittingly, I had been guilty of proof texting again. Yet instead of pulling just one verse out of context, I lifted an entire paragraph from the page and placed it floating in space. The Letter to the Romans, Paul's greatest theological work, can rarely be understood in small snippets of text. It is a grand narrative, both abstract and personal, being woven by Paul as he looks out upon the daily debauchery and idolatry in the Greek city of Corinth. When we read Romans 1, beginning in verse 18, Paul makes his case in a very linear fashion about what he is witnessing, but we need to fill in a few blanks to connect all of the theological dots.

Paul Explains a Descent into Sin

First, God's wrath is revealed for those who suppress truth. From the text alone, we can tell that this is directed toward pagan gentiles, since Paul pivots in Romans 2 to address Jews as also under God's judgment. This has been the uncontested traditional understanding of how Paul engaged his mixed non-Jewish and Jewish audience.

More specifically, however, Paul would have been writing Romans 1 in response to the people who worked in the 12 or so pagan temples and the profitable religious industry that revolved around these temples. This economic sector employed thousands of people in Corinth, everyone from the temple priests to the craftsmen who made the idols. The Temple of Aphrodite alone was said to have once had a thousand prostitutes for sexual rituals when the Greeks controlled the city, and the practices continued in lesser forms into the Romanized first century[37].

Needless to say, these are not the kind of people who would honor or thank God, even though they practiced religion. In fact, Paul found out firsthand in the nearby city of Ephesus that the leaders of the pagan religious industry would try to kill Christians who brought the Gospel into their cities and negatively impacted their businesses. These people, with minds increasingly darkened, exchanged the glory of God for the paltry idols carved out in the image of people and animals.

Now comes an important shift in Paul's narrative. With darkened minds and while worshiping idols, participants in these pagan temples and cults find before them a path to begin descending into sexual depravity, Paul explains. They act out their lusts and dishonor their bodies. This depravity then devolves further into homosexual acts, where both worshipers and temple workers—notice the text says, "*their* women"—also begin to engage in homosexual acts with each other.

These sinners then receive the "due penalty" for their sin, a phrase about which theologians have only been able to make guesses. Some have inferred that it is a reference to male worshipers castrating themselves in a cultic frenzy, something that did actually occur in the ancient world[38]. Others have mused that it is loss of gender identity or even more absurdly, a prophetic reference to AIDS. Perhaps the least controversial suggestion is that because it is placed so late in Paul's narrative, it is simply a hinting that the "due penalty" is spiritual separation from God, since Paul will later say in his letter to the Romans that "the wages of sin is death."

Finally, Paul details the wicked icing on the cake. These same debased people fall into a laundry list of other heavy sins as a result, ranging from disobeying their parents to murder.

If we were to summarize Paul's chronology of the wickedness he's observing in the city of Corinth, it would look something like this:

- **Suppression of the truth and refusing to honor or thank God leads to...**
- **A darkening of the mind,**
  which leads to...
- **Exchanging any worship of God for worship of idols,**
  which leads to...
- **Lusts and sexually dishonoring one's body,**
  which leads to...
- **Homosexual attraction and homosexual acts,**
  which leads to...
- **Increasingly more varied forms of sin.**

This is a complex descent into sin, but what should be very clear for any reader in the chronology and context of Paul's narrative in Romans 1 is that this has absolutely nothing to do with same-sex relationships. This is not an ambiguous, generalized portrayal of non-Christians. Paul is painting a picture of the pagan religious industry and its consumers. This likely was epitomized by either the Temple of Aphrodite itself or a Cybeline cult in Corinth. The former had its prostitution ring that would have operated in the temple or around the city, while the latter actually hosted orgies of men and women who mutilated their sex organs to achieve a state of "genderless transcendence."[39]

Moreover, Paul is speaking specifically about people who have rejected God, worship idols, are consumed with lust and love sin. That we would apply the reasoning of this passage to all people with a homosexual orientation, including people who love Jesus, makes a mockery of Paul's careful logic. Given that I believe Paul is divinely inspired by the Holy Spirit, I am incredibly hesitant to believe that Paul mistakenly thought all same-sex attraction was the product of wanton depravity.

Heterosexuals Practicing Homosexuality

But what about Paul detailing the homosexual behavior of men and women as "dishonorable," "shameless," and "contrary to nature?" Surely we can't ignore that just because Paul is addressing the moral corruption that comes with pagan temple cults around him. We should not, but we also should not ignore the other key words in the very same sentence. Paul also describes their homosexuality as a result of "passions," essentially unbridled lust and desire. Yet have you ever heard a gay man or lesbian woman tell you he or she discovered their same-sex orientation via an insatiable lust leading him or her to that realization? I never have, nor have I ever heard of any empirical data that might suggest this.

Even more critical to Paul's context is that Paul identifies all this homosexual activity to initially heterosexual idolaters. In the verses prior Paul describes the heterosexual sex ceremonies these people were having, which is why he also includes the critical caveat that both these men and women either gave up or exchanged "natural relations for what is contrary to nature." Fitting within the ancient Mediterranean worldview that often viewed homosexuality as excessive and uncontrolled sexual desire by otherwise heterosexual people, Paul essentially saw them as straight people having gay sex. So whether applying ancient categories or contemporary categories of same-sex sexuality, Paul is still right that this is very unnatural.

In the same vein, we would be careless to expand the scope of Paul's condemnation to those people with deeply rooted and enduring same-sex orientations, expressing sexual affection for those they love. Just as we saw with the Sodom and Gomorrah story, where homosexual gang-rape by heterosexual men does not constitute a valid analysis of same-sex relationships, it would be equally dishonest for us to smuggle any bias against LGBT people into Romans. Heterosexuals engaging in homosexual acts during the worship of pagan gods, which bears an uncanny resemblance to the Levitical context, has no logical bearing on same-sex relationships.

Am I then saying that Paul would have endorsed same-sex relationships? Probably not. Paul's formative exposure to homosexuality was limited to older men engaged in sexual relationships with younger boys (i.e. pederasty), temple prostitution, and wild temple cultic orgies. Additionally, as a former Jewish Pharisee in the first century, Paul was culturally predisposed to scorn expressions of homosexuality. Yet just as we excuse Paul's acceptance of slavery (Colossians 3:22) based on his ancient cultural and religious context, we should also be very careful to import his experience with expressions of first-century homosexuality into our current context of loving and monogamous same-sex relationships.

Does this view still maintain the authority of Scripture? Definitely. The Bible's authority is upheld strictly insomuch as it pertains to the scope that it definitively addresses. However, even more theologically conservative Christians would agree that Scriptural authority should not be extended in the same way to issues that author did not intend to address.

Obviously, the discussion about the biblical ethics surrounding homosexuality does not end here. Yet this analysis of Romans' context, coupled with the previous chapter's debunking of clobber passages, should put to rest the uncritical notion that the Bible specifically condemns same-sex relationships.

Chapter Five

Other Attempts to Condemn Same-Sex Relationships

As non-inclusive Christians become more familiar with the scholarship that strongly indicates the Bible does not condemn same-sex relationships, they have begun to split on their strategy to defend their traditional position. One tactic is simply to categorically deny the textual and cultural evidence at almost every point[40]. For every exegetically sound deconstruction of the aforementioned clobber passages, a non-inclusive theologian will find a way to refute it—some with more intellectual honesty than others.

However, I have observed that this fight over the

Other Attempts to Condemn Same-Sex Relationships 65

Greek and cultural context is no longer being pursued by non-inclusive Christians as the winning strategy, for the simple reason that it's not working. The growing new approach is to formulate condemnations of same-sex relationships that are derived from Scripture, but are more subject to creative interpretation than a direct clobber verse is. I have encountered three major attempts at this. For example, Matthew 19:3-12:

> *And Pharisees came up to him and tested him by asking, "Is it lawful to divorce one's wife for any cause?" He answered, "Have you not read that he who created them from the beginning made them male and female, and said, 'Therefore a man shall leave his father and his mother and hold fast to his wife, and the two shall become one flesh'? So they are no longer two but one flesh. What therefore God has joined together, let not man separate." They said to him, "Why then did Moses command one to give a certificate of divorce and to send her away?" He said to them, "Because of your hardness of heart Moses allowed you to divorce your wives, but from the beginning it was not so. And I say to you: whoever divorces his wife, except for sexual immorality, and marries another, commits adultery."*
>
> *The disciples said to him, "If such is the case of a man with his wife, it is better not to marry." But he said to them, "Not everyone can receive this saying, but only those to whom it is given. For there are eunuchs who have been so from birth, and there are eunuchs who have been made eunuchs by men, and there are eunuchs who have made themselves eunuchs for the sake of the kingdom of heaven. Let the one, who is*

able to receive this, receive it." (ESV)

This is an interesting passage on multiple levels, but in the context of our discussion, it's particularly troublesome because some non-inclusive Christians attempt to bring Jesus into the battle to condemn same-sex relationships. The argument here is fairly straightforward. Jesus affirms marriage as being between a man and woman, and appeals to the beginning of creation in the process; ergo, Jesus' definition of marriage logically disqualifies homosexuals from relationships.

Even for the most conservative evangelical, the problems with this line of thinking should be obvious. Jesus is clearly not making an argument *for* heterosexuality. No one in the story is questioning heterosexuality. The Pharisees essentially want to know if it's morally acceptable to divorce an aging or annoying wife and upgrade to a newer model. Jesus is making a beautiful argument that we should all affirm, but that argument is for the sacredness of relational and sexual commitment within the marriage covenant.

Ethically speaking, I would strongly caution any non-inclusive Christian from giving into the temptation to use Jesus as a rhetorical tool for a topic such as this. Given that so many gays and lesbians feel rejected by God, invoking Jesus' name against same-sex relationships can only further that perception. Plus, Jesus doesn't even remotely come close to doing this. Debating Paul's meaning in Romans 1 is a fair fight.

Hijacking Jesus' words into a weapon for condemnation of same-sex relationships borders on blasphemous.

Eunuchs and Marriage

What is often ignored in this passage, though, is Jesus' response when the disciples comment that marriage might be too hard for them. Jesus goes on about these "eunuchs" not being able to marry, which is not exactly an identifier we use nowadays. Eunuchs, most inclusively defined in Biblical times, can best be described as men who were not heterosexually active. This was done often as part of dedicating their life to a cause, leader, or government, believing that sexual abstinence (either by choice or through physical castration) allowed for greater dedication and loyalty. Some eunuchs also participated in homosexuality because of their self-castration, but this seems to have been limited primarily to cultic priests[41].

Regardless, Jesus describes three eunuchs: those who were born eunuchs, those who were made eunuchs by men, and those who made themselves eunuchs for the kingdom of Heaven. The third is clearly a description of something like a Catholic priest. The second likely refers either to dedication to a leader or the loss of a man's genitals in battle. The first of the three is fairly cryptic. Nonetheless, you would be hard pressed to find a historian who would tell you Jesus is referring to men who were born with ambiguous genitalia[42]. More moderate and liberal Christian scholars conclude that the only logical and practical translation of someone who is born a eunuch, or someone born with a non-heterosexual disposition, is a homosexual.

If this is the accurate understanding of the first category of eunuch, this passage indicates that many gays or lesbians are born homosexual and that their orientation is not of their choosing. This is an important realization about human sexuality to be sure, but not necessarily a realization that requires much persuasion as it did even a decade ago.

Yet if this eunuch category does indeed refer to a homosexual orientation, it actually creates another potential conundrum, since Jesus is talking about who *should not* be married and instead should live a life of sexual abstinence. When I was convinced same-sex relationships were sinful, I actually made the argument that while sexual orientation was innate, it was a sign that God was calling that person to a life of singleness, and likely to a life of service to the Kingdom of God. It was like the third category that Jesus appears to name, that of a voluntary Catholic priest, minus the voluntary part.

The hole in my logic was merely a less noticeable one than we find in the argument that, because Jesus affirmed marriage, he was implicitly forbidding same-sex relationships. In the first century, marriage was chiefly about passing down wealth and the creating families who could also pass down that wealth. Romance wasn't high on the list of priorities. As a result, same-sex relationships, while existing in various forms in the ancient world, never culminated in legal marriages. Even the Emperor Nero's bizarre attempt at marrying a castrated boy was mocked by his contemporaries[43]. At that time, it was antithetical to the culture's central purpose of marriages.

So when Jesus says "born" eunuchs are not going to get married, this is a descriptive statement about the nature of marriage in that day. For reasons of procreation and property, same-sex marriage wasn't an option on the cultural table. Yet there is nothing in Jesus' words that should lead us to think he was making a prescriptive statement that homosexuals, while born that way, should never get married for the rest of human history.

It would be just as equally mistaken to say that because Jesus makes references to slaves (Luke 12:47-48), Jesus prescriptively affirms slavery. No Christian today believes this because we all realize that Jesus references slavery descriptively, using language that reflected the first-century culture into which he was incarnated. So if we don't read Jesus prescriptively when he mentions slaves, it would be equally unwise of us to read Jesus prescriptively when he descriptively mentions that marriage only existed for heterosexual couples.

Sullying the Bride of Christ

What makes arguments like these so much more effective than those that simply rely on dubious Greek translations and proof texting is that they are not subject to the ground rules of typical biblical scholarship. Take, for example, these two passages that refer to the "bride of Christ."

> *Husbands, love your wives, as Christ loved the church and gave himself up for her, that he might sanctify her, having cleansed her by the washing of water with the word, so that he might present the church to himself in splendor, without spot or wrinkle or any such thing, that she might be holy and without blemish. In the same way husbands should love their wives as their own bodies. He who loves his wife loves himself. For no one ever hated his own flesh, but nourishes and cherishes it, just as Christ does the church, because we are members of his body. "Therefore a man shall leave his father and mother and hold fast to his wife, and the two shall become one flesh." This mystery is profound, and I am saying that it refers to Christ and the church. However, let each one of you love his wife as himself, and let the wife see that she respects her husband.*
> *– Ephesians 5:25-27 (ESV)*

> *And I saw the holy city, New Jerusalem, coming down out of heaven from God, prepared as a bride adorned for her husband.*
> *– Revelation 21:2 (ESV)*

Even when I was adamantly opposed to same-sex relationships, I grimaced at referencing these passages as evidence that God condemns homosexuality. The rationale is that Jesus is described as the husband of the universal Church, which itself is described as the bride. By applying this obvious metaphor in the most literal way possible, the conclusion is that same-

Other Attempts to Condemn Same-Sex Relationships 71

sex relationships are sinful because Jesus is not marrying a metaphorical man. Not only are they sinful, but because God uses bride and groom language to describe Christ's relationship to his Church, same-sex relationships are actually one of the greatest perversions of God's design.

This is not a line of thinking that comes out of rural fundamentalist churches either. The first time I ever heard this appropriation of the bride of Christ metaphor used to condemn homosexuality, it was taught by a pastor from one of the largest mega-churches in the country. Logically this is an anti-gay metaphor that is easily debunked for all sorts of reasons of context, not to mention that this Church that will be wed to Christ will contain some men in it (or so I hope).

Yet, this argument against gays and lesbians is not meant to be a logical, properly exegeted application of Scripture. It paints a visually striking image that plays on latent or openly homophobic prejudices in imagining Jesus marrying a man. It's compelling, and dangerously so, because it requires no knowledge of Greek or historical context while returning to the notion that any expression of homosexuality is actually in a special category of uniquely bad sins.

Like when Jesus affirms lifelong marriage, what is again tragic here is that some non-inclusive Christians have let their agenda drive their interpretation of what are otherwise beautiful metaphors. The bride of Christ imagery was not originally used to teach Christians about why only opposite-sex marriage is moral, but rather about Christ's covenantal, sacrificial, and unending love for his people. Therefore, we should not be forced to choose from celebrating same-sex marriage and celebrating the future reality of Christ's eternal marriage to the Church. These are not at odds with one another. That is clearly not the implication of the text.

Same-sex marriage does nothing to undermine the bride of Christ metaphor, but rather by the covenantal nature of marriage, affirms the very essence of it. What actually undermines this imagery is a culture of live-in relationships, divorce, and inflexible doctrines that label otherwise covenantal, sacrificial, and unending romantic commitments as sinful. How tragic that some Christians have taken what God meant for encouragement, hope, and joy, and sullied the beautiful bride of Christ with anti-gay overtones.

No Adam and Steve or Barbeque?

These roundabout attacks on same-sex relationships are, however, still overshadowed by the appeal to Genesis 2:18-24, a more sophisticated version of the argument that "God made Adam and Eve, not Adam and Steve."

> *Then the Lord God said, "It is not good that the man should be alone; I will make him a helper fit for him." Now out of the ground the Lord God had formed every beast of the field and every bird of the heavens and brought them to the man to see what he would call them. And whatever the man called every living creature, that was its name. The man gave names to*

Other Attempts to Condemn Same-Sex Relationships 73

> *all livestock and to the birds of the heavens and to every beast of the field. But for Adam there was not found a helper fit for him. So the Lord God caused a deep sleep to fall upon the man, and while he slept took one of his ribs and closed up its place with flesh. And the rib that the Lord God had taken from the man he made into a woman and brought her to the man. Then the man said, "This at last is bone of my bones and flesh of my flesh; she shall be called Woman, because she was taken out of Man." Therefore a man shall leave his father and his mother and hold fast to his wife, and they shall become one flesh. (ESV)*

Beyond the initial creation of man and woman as intimately designed for each other, conservative theologians say that what makes this passage unique is that it addresses the original ideals for humanity's sexuality and relationships. God literally made man and woman for each other. They are the perfect companions and compliments for one another. At the very least, same-sex partners are anatomically inferior to God's perfect design of heterosexuality.

There is a bit of Platonism undergirding this thought, that is, the philosophy that posits that perfect forms of everything exist. Perfect love, perfect heroism, perfect chairs—literally all of existence reflecting from an ideal essence. Similarly then, heterosexuality is the most perfect form of sexuality. Platonism isn't exactly "biblical," since the philosophy came from the mind of a pagan named Plato. That being said, appealing to the pre-Fall state of the world in the Garden of Eden as a standard of perfection is an approach often used by Christians, both conservative and liberal.

For example, it's common for Christians to acknowledge that while disease infects our bodies now, it wasn't so before humanity rebelled against God in Eden. So when we pray for physical healing, we are really praying for God to make our bodies more in line with a pre-Fall state of being. Just about any discord in human relationships falls under this heading as well, which is why we believe that at least in large part, Christ is redeeming our post-Fall lifestyles and nature to a more pre-Fall way of living and being.

So when non-inclusive Christians say that, according to our accounts in Genesis, heterosexuality is God's original design, I'm inclined to agree. Anatomy does speak to compatibility and purpose. My Roman Catholic friends have a point that "Natural Law," or the process of determining purpose from observing nature itself, can provide some clues to God's intent. So while I am open to the possibility that same-sex orientations are part of God's diverse creation in a way that is akin to racial diversity, it is still difficult for me to conceive of homosexuality as part of God's perfect plan for humanity.

There are just too many aspects about it that don't seem ideal, even beyond non-complimentary anatomy. No ability, outside modern fertility technology, to produce children. Though socially influenced, more mirrored gender traits rather than complimentary gender traits. Or how about only having an available partner pool, given what we know about the average makeup of homosexuals in a given town, of about 1.5 to 3 percent of a population? Those are not good odds.

It is important though to note that there is a distinct difference between any disadvantages caused by a homosexual orientation and whether any harm is actually caused by acting on it. Being disadvantaged from the Fall doesn't mean attempts to seek happiness within the parameters of that disadvantage are necessarily sinful. We are all born with some disadvantages from the Fall, be it with a disease, in poverty, or under oppression. Yet, good theology has historically never ordered people to permanently accept and suffer from their disadvantage. It is not a sin for the deaf to learn to communicate through sign language. It is not a sin for the poor to enjoy any luxury normally reserved for the rich. It is not a sin for the second-class citizen to work toward political equality. Why then is it a sin for someone with a homosexual orientation to pursue romantic relationships?

If the rebuttal is still a return to God's original design, please realize that I understand the hesitation. Even though we can't be sure about what God's original design was with regards to sexual orientation, I grant that it does seem unlikely that homosexuality was part of God's original plan for humanity.

But then again, neither was eating meat.

Think about it. The Bible says that there was no death in the Garden of Eden and that Adam and Eve only ate fruits and vegetables (and perhaps a few legumes), but definitely no meat. The first time an animal dies is when God sacrifices an animal to make clothing for Adam and Eve. The first time we hear of people eating meat is when we read about Adam and Eve's sons, Cain and Abel. If the Garden of Eden is our baseline for God's "Plan A," and if, as redeemed followers of Jesus we are called to model a pre-Fall humanity, we would also have to admit that eating meat is intrinsically sinful. There may be some liberal theologians who would embrace this line of reasoning to its vegetarian conclusion, but I've never met a non-inclusive theologian who thought eating any kind of meat was a sin. Even liberal theologians aren't advocating a return to nudism, because that would be pre-Fall as well.

Nor can we look to the new Heaven and the new Earth as described by Jesus or in Revelation to set the standard of what our sexuality will be one day. In fact, Jesus himself in Mark 12:25 rejects the notion that when God returns to renew and restore the planet, our sexuality will be expressed the way it is now:

> *For when [people] rise from the dead, they neither marry nor are given in marriage, but are like angels in heaven. (ESV)*

So if some post-Fall behavior is considered entirely moral by Scripture, and God's return to Earth does not necessitate a complete reversal to life in the Garden of Eden, it should be evident

Other Attempts to Condemn Same-Sex Relationships 77

that not all consequences of the Fall are inherently sinful. They may not be ideal, but not meeting the platonic paradigm of perfection is not the equivalent of evil.

But what about the biblical regulations regarding post-Fall realities? True, there may be plenty of post-Fall situations that are less than ideal, but biblical laws and codes take those into account. You can eat meat, but there are kosher rules for how it is to be prepared. You can wear clothes, but there are guidelines on modesty. You can even divorce, but there are specific conditions that need to be met to permit two Christians to separate. Nowhere though do we find any regulations about same-sex relationships. There are no conditions listed in the Bible that would permit it under any circumstance. Therefore, this must mean that no expression of homosexuality is ever permissible in God's eyes.

However, consider how incredibly rare homosexuality was within the Hebrew community, which celebrated large families to the point of cultural idolatry (take, for example, Genesis 30:19-24). Even later within the more hedonistic Greco-Roman culture, lifelong same-sex relationships were generally unheard of. Just as the Bible doesn't give us regulations on modern dating, since dating didn't exist in the ancient world, we should not expect the Bible to give us regulations on same-sex relationships. Heterosexual courting or arranged marriages were the cultural norm in which the Bible spoke into. This is a limited scope of cultural practice that Christians today readily acknowledge on a number of issues, apart from homosexuality. But if we're honest, the absence of guidelines for gay and lesbian people in the Bible cannot logically entail that the God must not recognize their need for romantic relationships.

Seeking Real Redemption

When pastors preach about us not living up to "God's best for us," this is about God's will for us individually and derived from God's intimate knowledge of our situations. While virtue may be measured in comparison to the perfection of God, sin is not. We judge the sinfulness of a behavior not by whether it measures up to a theoretical level of idealism, but by whether we fail God's expectations for us or whether we directly or indirectly cause harm to ourselves and others. Yes, we all are spiritually, physically and psychologically broken from the Fall. We are all in need of spiritual, physical and psychological redemption once we are justified in Jesus' atonement for our sin. That redemption means, as Paul said, dying to our old self and becoming a new creation in Christ. Those who have homosexual orientations are no exception.

However, perhaps what needs to be redeemed, what needs to die, is not homosexuality. Perhaps this redemption that comes through the sanctification of the Holy Spirit is meant by God to be found uniquely elsewhere.

Chapter Six

The Biblical Foundation for Same-Sex Relationships

An important part of my evolution in coming to biblical terms with same-sex relationships was to understand how homosexuality could fit within the context of a biblical worldview. This is important because the inevitable rebuttal to a successful deconstruction of every single "biblical" attack on homosexuality is almost always a demand to show where the Bible affirms same-sex relationships. If the Bible can't explicitly affirm homosexuality, then it's probably still a sin, or so the rationale goes.

This logic of course breaks down very quickly once you realize, as I did, that we very often don't apply this high of a standard to much of our own lives. The Bible affirms theocracy and monarchy, not democracy, yet we clearly prefer democracy. The Bible affirms courtship, not dating, but few Christians have a problem with premarital dates and even kissing. Jesus and the early Church affirmed pacifism, not war, but almost all Christians today recognize that sometimes war, while still a last resort, is necessary.

There will not be any verses in Scripture that explicitly affirm same-sex relationships for the same reason Scripture doesn't affirm democracy: neither really existed in ancient Middle Eastern culture. Yes, mob rule occurred, but that is hardly democracy. Yes, homosexual orgies and male-to-male rapes occurred, but that is hardly same-sex marriage.

While there have been some attempts in recent years to identify homosexual relationships between the future King David and his boyhood friend Jonathan, between Ruth and Naomi, and between a Roman centurion and his servant whom Jesus encounters, most of these efforts are forced to deal with very scant Scriptural evidence. They may indeed be true, particularly the relationship between David and Jonathan, but they still require a good deal of speculation.

Moreover, when I was first presented with these alleged examples of biblically affirmed homosexual behavior, at a time when I was still convinced of the sinfulness of same-sex relationships, my response was one of offense. I found it revolting that someone was willing to interject a modern Western conception of homosexuality into an ancient Middle Eastern culture that made space for comfortable expressions of non-sexual affection between men. If anything, these arguments slowed down my theological journey to reconsidering the non-inclusive doctrines on homosexuality.

Companionship and Forced Singleness

For the two reasons, mentioned above, and for the sake of brevity, I will not rely on finding LGBT characters in the Bible to prove the Bible's potential affirmation of same-sex relationships. Furthermore, I also don't really think it's necessary.

Let's first return to the Genesis 2:18:

> *Then the Lord God said, "It is not good that the man should be alone; I will make him a helper fit for him." (ESV)*

These few words by the author of this creation story are, I believe, the key to turning the theological tide toward biblical legitimacy for same-sex relationships. Why? Because while the Lord God never says that homosexuality is not good in creation accounts, there is one condition that is unequivocally labeled "not good"—forced singleness[44].

Adam is created spiritually and physically whole,

but he is without a companion. Despite Adam being in the very presence of God, God still believes Adam needs a flesh-and-bones relationship. A quasi-comical scene then ensues as Adam tries to determine whether one of the animals might make a suitable companion, but to no avail. God ultimately solves the problem of the first man's forced singleness with the creation of the first woman.

But what if a man isn't attracted to a woman, but only other men? What if a woman isn't attracted to a man, but only other women? For the reasons we covered earlier this isn't fundamentally ideal. Yet given that the absence of companionship for Adam is declared "not good" by God even before the very existence of Eve, how can the biblical solution for someone with a same-sex orientation be requiring a lifetime of celibacy? How can a life of forced singleness be, as many non-inclusive pastors have glibly said, "God's best for them"? How does this square with Jesus' commandment that we "desire mercy, not sacrifice" when interpreting Scripture? In the very least, forced singleness directly contradicts God's desire for humanity according to Genesis.

If one finds this too abstract though, Paul makes our choice abundantly practical. Paul tells us in 1 Corinthians 3:9 regarding single people and celibacy,

> *"But if they cannot exercise self-control, they should marry. For it is better to marry than to burn with passion." (ESV)*

Paul, himself a vocal proponent of celibacy, had no desireto force such a command on those not inclined to it. Marriage, even a marriage in less than ideal circumstances, was preferable. It is not hard to imagine how this might be equally applicable to gays and lesbians. One may not find homosexuality ideal, but based on Paul's very logic, it may very well be better for a homosexual person to marry someone of the same sex than to burn with passion for as long as his or her hormones keep flickering. Yet if our Christian response to homosexuality is still to unflinchingly forbid marriage for homosexuals, then we are simply ignoring the cautions of Scripture.

Now, could a homosexual who accepts the reality of his or her orientation still feel a call to celibacy? Yes, and for those LGBT people who feel called to abstain from expressing their sexuality, I see no reason on the surface to question that conviction. Nor do I question heterosexuals who feel that same call to celibacy. But, if we are even willing to consider that homosexuality may not be sinful, Genesis 2:18 and Corinthians 3:9 should challenge us to realize that affirming same-sex relationships is preferable to a doctrine that violates God's values.

Same-sex relationships may not fit the pre-Fall ideal, but even prior to God's pairing of Adam and Eve, God created the fundamental human need for companionship. So when Christians acknowledge the validity of same-sex relationships, we honor the good and edifying desire to share romantic intimacy that was first placed in a person's heart by the Creator Himself.

The Effects of Sin

It would be theologically reckless to affirm same-sex relationships, though, on the sole basis of Genesis 2:18. It's important that we also consider the effects of affirming same-sex relationships, because whether it is sin or an acceptable moral choice, the spiritual fruit of it should correspond with our theological position. What I mean by this is that if you believe same-sex relationships are sinful, then there must be tangible evidence available that engaging in such a relationship is harmful. Or if you believe same-sex relationships are not sinful, then you must demonstrate that there are no negative effects, spiritual or otherwise, from engaging in one.

This is a very important point. Scripture tells us that sin damages us. In Isaiah 59:2, the prophet tells the people of Israel that "your iniquities have made a separation between you and your God, and your sins have hidden his face from you so that he does not hear." On some level, every unrepentant or un-confessed sin creates separation between a person and God. Consequently, Isaiah indicates that this also adversely affects a person's prayers. In the New Testament, 1 John 1:6 reaffirms this spiritual cause-and-effect when the author says, "If we say we have fellowship with him while we walk in darkness, we lie and do not practice the truth."

It doesn't stop there, though. Since God explicitly

points to himself as the source of peace (Philippians 4:7) and joy (John 1:4), then all sin that inherently reduces our intimacy with God will also inherently rob us of some of our peace and joy. In fact, sin draws us to physical and spiritual death. Romans 6:23 goes so far as to as to say, "The wages of sin is death."

If we're ever struggling to understand whether a choice is sinful or not because Scripture doesn't seem to clearly condemn or affirm it, God has not left us to be trapped in endless exegetical debate. Sin is not merely an abstract concept, but a reality that manifests concretely in the world's daily brokenness. We can call sin "sin" even without a specific Bible passage if we can show causation between the potential sin in question and the harmful effects. According to the Bible, sin will show itself for what is, both individually and societally.

So here is a simple question. What are some harmful effects of a same-sex relationship that is modeled after every biblical guideline for an opposite-sex relationship?

Even when I thought same-sex relationships were sinful, my argument rested on my interpretation of Scripture and not on my interpretation of reality. I could not muster up a single coherent harmful effect of homosexuality.

That's not to say I didn't try. At first I pointed to the constantly referenced "gay lifestyle" as proof that homosexuality was spiritually destructive. I soon realized though that the "gay lifestyle," a phrase most associated with casual sexual encounters, was little different from the partying and boozing "straight lifestyle" that I had observed at college. Homosexuality wasn't the culprit. Directionless sexuality, loneliness, and lust were behind any "hook-up" culture. It was clearly a case of correlation and not causation.

If there was any causation to be noted, it was that we should not be surprised to find a more promiscuous bent within segments of any culture that has been essentially exiled from one of the last American institutions that teaches sexual purity and lifetime monogamy. If monogamous relationships are lacking in some in the gay community, it may point directly back to the absence of the Christian community. Either way, I admitted I couldn't fairly pin the harmful effects of promiscuity on some attribute intrinsic to the nature of same-sex relationships.

Similarly, I tried to make a case that gay parenting was bad for children. It seemed self evident that kids needed a mother and a father, and that anything less would be harmful to the child in question. However, I first realized that being adopted by loving gay or lesbian parents was obviously preferable to not being adopted at all. Then I realized that showing causation between same-sex parents and their children's well-being would be difficult to accurately establish.

Nonetheless, both those for and against same-sex marriage have understandably attempted it. In 2012, a study by a non-inclusive Catholic professor funded by anti-gay organizations produced the first in-depth study that attempted to show a harmful causation. However, its methodology was quickly shown as fatally flawed, primarily because it compared children mostly raised in broken homes who had seen some sort of parental same-sex relationship to children mostly raised in stable heterosexual households[45]. The data was crafted to highlight the worst possible conditions. Meanwhile, every other study for over twenty years has confirmed a different conclusion: that children raised by same-sex parents are no worse off than children raised by opposite-sex parents[46]. In fact, one of the most recent and thorough studies has revealed they may actually do better[47].

Sexual Reductionism

Faced with a dwindling reservoir of social arguments against same-sex relationships, I even attempted to argue that the evidentiary proof of homosexuality's sinfulness was that anal sex was harmful. Granted, I'm not a doctor, but I still think this can be true for those who engage in it with enough frequency. However, the problem with this so-called consequence of homosexuality is that it is hardly an exclusive consequence of homosexuality. Heterosexuals are just as capable of engaging in anal sex, a sex act that has found pastoral approval by even such conservative evangelicals as Mark Driscoll[48]. Moreover, it is hardly an applicable sexual practice for half the homosexual population. No one has ever accused lesbian sex of being physically harmful. So if we're using anal sex as proof of a spiritually degraded condition, lesbians are off the hook and those pastors who are more conservative than the likes of Mark Driscoll may need to start interviewing their heterosexual married congregants about the specific details of their sex lives.

Beyond inaccurately singling out the potentially negative physical effects of a particular sexual act as representative of all homosexual relationships, criticizing sexuality on the basis of one sex act is also a terribly reductionist approach to sexuality. Sexual pleasure between partners, including same-sex partners, can be experienced through an incredible variety of ways, just as with heterosexual partners.

Besides, most of the ways in which a couple can share sexual intimacy were originally "gross" to us as at one point, which I suspect is often an unspoken reason behind the evangelical objection to male anal sex. Recall when you thought at age 5 that kissing was gross, or the horror you experienced when you watched your first "sex-ed" video in grade school. Those heterosexual sexual acts were gross to us then. Yet, over time—the stalwart 17th century Puritans among us notwithstanding—our perceptions changed significantly in just a few years.

As any married couple should be able to confess, our sex lives can be altogether awkward, intimate, scary, beautiful, frustrating, hilarious, and wonderful. How odd it is, then, that some non-inclusive Christians have tried to judge the sex lives of every single gay and lesbian. Our personal comfort or discomfort with a particular sex act at a given moment can't be a measure of its morality, much less the moral sum of a relationship.

Still, to focus so much on homosexual sex itself is too reductionist from a biblical perspective. To be made in the *imago Dei*, the image of God, means we are more than just our anatomy. Our romantic relationships should not be reduced to the methods by which we receive and give sexual pleasure. That is far more a value of an unbelieving world than of a biblical worldview. It doesn't honor the reality that we were made to reflect the wonderful complexities of God's self. Instead, reducing people to how sexual parts fit or don't fit is dehumanizing. In taking a biblical approach to sexuality, romantic relationships and how we express our affection within those relationships should be evaluated holistically for their spiritual healthiness.

The Effects of Virtue

Looking to Scripture again, we are blessed with timeless clarity about what healthy relationships look like. In 1 Corinthians 13:4-8 and 13, the Apostle Paul famously describes the marks of Godly love.

> *Love is patient and kind; love does not envy or boast; it is not arrogant or rude. It does not insist on its own way; it is not irritable or resentful; it does not rejoice at wrongdoing, but rejoices with the truth. Love bears all things, believes all things, hopes all things, endures all things. Love never ends...So now faith,*

hope, and love abide, these three; but the greatest of these is love. (ESV)

While it should be noted Paul wasn't directly referring to romantic relationships in this passage, for millennia the Church has felt comfortable appropriating Paul's words for the context of marriage. In contrast to whatever definition the world may offer us, this is what God tells us defines healthy love.

Even the staunchest critic of same-sex relationships would be unlikely to say gay and lesbian couples don't love each other. They may say they're misguided, broken, and confused, but it's hard to deny they are attempting to love their significant other. So here is the point of tension if one believes same-sex relationships are indeed sinful. How can we label any relationship as sinful, if it approaches God's difficult and exhaustive standard for healthy relationships? If we believe this, we are forced into a tenuous, if not contradictory position. Even if the love in a same-sex relationship bears every single mark of biblical love, it is somehow, in some way, not biblical. And not only is it not biblical, it's actually sinful.

Do you see the problem here? To condemn same-sex relationships as sinful requires us to altogether ignore the guidance of Scripture for determining healthy relationships or to acknowledge that same-sex relationships can appear to be healthy even by biblical standards, but are imperceptibly destructive.

The most committed, and often most educated non-inclusive Christians, will also try to take refuge in a pseudo-spiritual circular argument about sin. Perhaps same-sex relationships are guilty of the sin of "eschatological impatience,"[49] since those in them are unwilling to wait until Christ's Second Coming where they will be healed of their homosexuality and wed with God. In other words, the evidence of harm is so non-existent that one must accuse LGBT people of an esoteric type of sin that can only be proven false when the world ends. With this kind of theology, one can't help but wonder if runaway slaves in pre-Civil War America were eschatologically impatient, or if amputees today who impatiently use prosthetic limbs are guilty of this sin as well?

Still, sometimes the circle has only two points. It has even been said that the sinful effect of same-sex relationships is that it is intrinsically sinful, thereby needing no explanation of what harm it causes. Using what is known as a deontological approach, same-sex relationships become inherently "impure," "rebellious," "unnatural", or "idolatrous," since the Bible allegedly says so. Essentially, the harm caused by homosexuality is not an observable phenomenon and should have no bearing on our moral assessment of it. The harm caused by homosexuality is simply... homosexuality. That though, is not a logically passable argument. That is begging the question while simultaneously denying the Bible's clear teachings on the nature of sin and virtue.

The Fruit of the Spirit vs. Legalism

In his letters to the earliest churches, Paul is constantly admonishing Christians not to be legalistic in calling sin those things which are not sin (Colossians 2:20-23). There is a natural tendency within the human spirit to add man-made qualifiers to God's rules, especially when confronted with people whose lifestyles differ markedly from our own. The history of religion, in contrast to the Gospel, is littered with us-versus-them dichotomies, built from inventing new categories of sin. Religion gains power by identifying certain kinds of people or practices to condemn, meanwhile assuring that their own religious adherents can be thankful they aren't like "them."

Jesus himself warns against this effect of religion in the Gospel of Luke 18, with the parable of the tax collector and the Pharisee, but Paul's letter to the Galatians details how to determine if we are doing just that. The Galatian church is in conflict over whether various Mosaic laws—those laws that existed in Judaism—must be followed in order to be a good Christian (or perhaps even a Christian at all). As in the Corinthian passage, Paul counters with a straightforward and logical assessment that Christians should employ to determine whether their actions are in line with the Spirit of God:

> *But I say, walk by the Spirit, and you will not gratify the desires of the flesh. For the desires of the flesh are against the Spirit, and the desires of the Spirit are against the flesh, for these are opposed to each other,*

to keep you from doing the things you want to do.

But if you are led by the Spirit, you are not under the law. Now the works of the flesh are evident: sexual immorality, impurity, sensuality, idolatry, sorcery, enmity, strife, jealousy, fits of anger, rivalries, dissensions, divisions, envy, drunkenness, orgies, and things like these. I warn you, as I warned you before, that those who do such things will not inherit the kingdom of God. But the fruit of the Spirit is love, joy, peace, patience, kindness, goodness, faithfulness, gentleness, self-control; against such things there is no law.

– Galatians 5:16-23 (ESV)

Paul makes it abundantly clear that Christians should not label anything sin if it bears "fruit of the Spirit." Granted, assessing the fruit from a given behavior as healthy or unhealthy cannot be done flippantly. This takes careful and honest observation. However, once this is done, we cannot disregard it as an unreliable ethical measure since Paul specifically teaches it. Again, in the context of same-sex relationships, we can't supplant Paul's methodology for our own methodology in order to maintain a flimsy hold on any pet doctrine. Nor can we cynically claim that any fruit of the Spirit is a forgery if it happens to come from someone openly homosexual. Paul does not hold "false fruit" out as a legitimate caveat to his teaching in Galatians or elsewhere.

Can such a subjective standard become a slippery slope? Like many other doctrines in Christianity, of course. So let us then apply as high a standard as we would apply to heterosexual Christian marriages. If same-sex couples, both corporately and individually, are exhibiting love, joy, peace, patience, kindness, goodness, faithfulness, gentleness and self-control—as we see lived out in heterosexual Christian couples—how can we call homosexuality intrinsically sinful?

Yet, if we really believe that homosexuality is sinful *and* what the Bible says about the nature of sin is true, then same-sex relationships should yield the opposite of all these virtues. The relationship itself and the spiritual life of each individual participating in it should manifest the inescapable consequences of sin.

But unlike, say, the well-documented negative effects of premarital sex on teenagers[50], there exists virtually no empirical data to prove same-sex relationships are themselves emotionally destructive[51,52,53]. In fact, the data that does show higher risks of depression, suicide and promiscuity in some homosexuals can, with shocking regularity, often be traced to condemnation and exclusion at the hands of one's family, culture and churches[54].

The moment we meet an openly gay or lesbian person who loves Jesus and exhibits the fruit of Spirit, we must drop either our questionable belief that same-sex relationships must be sinful or abandon our orthodox belief that sin is spiritually and psychologically destructive. For while we could conceive of some sexual sins that could exist in a person's life alongside spiritual fruit, if same-sex relationships are indeed sinful, they would not be among them. Unrepentant same-sex relationships would be one of the most pervasive sins. Practically every aspect of the relationship, even its smallest expressions of affection, would be engaged in violating God's created order. Abundant spiritual fruit cannot coexist with unrepentant, pervasive sexual sin.

So even if we think the Bible may possibly condemn same-sex relationships, it seems nearly impossible to argue that the Bible doesn't really teach that sin is destructive. The clearest teaching of Scripture should always trump its more questionable interpretations. Otherwise, it borders on utter contempt of reason, biblical wisdom, and the well-being of a homosexual person's soul to say that though same-sex relationships may not function like biblical sin and even appear to be biblically virtuous, homosexuality is actually among the most insidious of sins.

I pray that is not the doctrinal path we will be willing to walk down, especially when a far better road for all people and a far better way for advancing the Gospel is before us. Based on our passages in Genesis, Corinthians and Galatians, a theology that takes in the whole counsel of Scripture would strongly indicate that same-sex relationships can be entirely acceptable to God and edifying to the individuals in the relationship.

Nor is this a pharisaical, abstract theology. This is a New Covenantal, practical theology carefully rooted in the human experience. It corresponds to reality when we let reality affirm, rather than undermine, God's truth. Once you read the testimonies of joyful Christian same-sex couples and come to know them personally as friends, the relevance and power of these scriptures will become increasingly evident.

A Redeemed Sexuality

So if homosexuality can be accepted by the spectrum of Scripture, both in the Old and New Testaments, what does it mean for the Spirit to redeem the sexuality of a gay or lesbian person? If the non-inclusive doctrine teaches that redemption must mean becoming asexual or somehow heterosexual is at least false if not spiritually harmful, what does biblical redemption in the sexuality of a homosexual look like?

Simple. The same as a biblical redemption in the sexuality of a heterosexual. An LGBT person would work to overcome the lust of the flesh for the self-control of the Spirit. He or she would use romantic affection not as a means of grasping for approval or love, but as a healthy reflection of the emotional and spiritual intimacy between two people. If there are places of brokenness for heterosexual people that need God's redemption, then there are places of brokenness for homosexual people that need God's redemption.

This is hardly a rejection of the biblical command to "take up one's cross" or "die to self." As any Christian heterosexual can attest to, successfully obeying commandments like these is difficult enough! Healthy sexuality for a LGBT person would face all the same challenges, and they would need the sanctifying work of the Spirit in order to be obedient. Yet those with homosexual orientations have one additional challenge in their lives that needs God's special provision and presence where those with a heterosexual orientation often do not.

Despair from fearing a life of forced singleness.

It's easy to forget as heterosexuals that we have pretty wide options when it comes to finding a spouse. Even Christians who bemoan the lack of Godly men or women to marry still have anywhere between 4.5 percent at worst and 26 percent at best of a potential population in a given city that may line up with their spiritual values[55]. Now consider that in your average town, gays and lesbians have only 1 to 3 percent of a given population that they can possibly date. Add being Christian to the formula and that number can easily drop to less than 1 percent. Those are not good odds.

Based on the greater difficulty of finding a compatible partner for homosexuals, especially those who are Christian, the temptation is much greater to fall into despair or settle for less than God's best. If we acknowledge that homosexuality is ultimately part of humanity's fallen state, we can see why this was a ripple effect of Adam and Eve's rebellion. Satan would love nothing more than the opposite of God's will that all people could find companionship.

The fall of humanity took perfect relationships and dashed them on the rocks of sin, splintering our hopes of edifying companionship into a fragment of a chance. The Evil One wants to create forced singleness and the despair that comes from fearing the possibility of it.

So when I say LGBT people must let God redeem them from despair and fear, I mean they must let God redeem them from being overwhelmed by the staggering odds and cultures that oppress them. In spite of these harsh realities, they can trust that God will not abandon them to a life of loneliness. God's provision, should God will it, is more than capable of providing an edifying spouse even for someone who finds the worldly odds are not in his or her favor. The Spirit redeems those with deeply rooted homosexual orientations from despair because the Spirit, when trusted, proves God faithful and gracious over and over again.

The temptation to despair for gays and lesbians is perhaps a burden far more common to them, but God's sovereignty is greater than despair. The daily redemption for homosexuals is that even if their orientation presents a myriad of additional difficulties, God provides a real and rational hope in relational provision. Rather than the unbiblical demands of forced singleness, this is the encouragement with which all Christians can provide their homosexual brothers and sisters with: *Jehovah Jireh*–the Lord will Provide.

Chapter Seven

Gay and Lesbian Christians and the Holy Spirit

Given that, for reasons already discussed, the biblical affirmation for same-sex relationships is limited, I find it important to flesh out a more holistic framework from Scripture. Included in the rest of the book are three other theological reasons that should give us additional comfort with the idea that same-sex relationships can conform to a life of obedience to Christ.

To begin, I feel we must account for the reality of the Holy Spirit and its efficacy in believers. How do we coherently reconcile the Spirit's role in the lives of those who have a same-sex orientation and who also claim a relationship with Christ? Can the Holy Spirit, with enough faith and prayer, allow someone to change their orientation? Also, for the sake of clarity, I'll be primarily referencing gays and lesbians in this conversation, but not bisexual or transgender people. Their testimonies are no less important, but are ones that I have less personal access to.

When I was convinced same-sex relationships were a sin, I tried to explain my position with a comparison to similar sins, chiefly alcoholism. The scientific data was beginning to become clear that homosexuality was not a "choice" in the sense that gays and lesbians choose their sexuality in any conscious way. There also existed reasonable data indicating that environmental and sociological factors were involved as well. To my understanding then, this made homosexuality most analogous to alcoholism. While an individual may make poor choices that lead to alcoholism, no one intentionally becomes an alcoholic. In most cases alcoholism is caused by a combination of genetic *and* environmental factors. Some people are highly susceptible to it, while others are far more resistant.

Similarly, it was becoming apparent to me that gays and lesbians, with a few highly touted exceptions, could not change their orientation. Through therapy, counseling and prayer, some seemed able to stop acting on their homosexual attractions. Even still, the men and women who had claimed to be successful examples of "conversion therapy," confessed continued struggles with the temptation of homosexuality. The parallel seemed to match alcoholism as well. Alcoholics are never cured. They are only perpetually recovering. We've all heard the stories of someone who struggles with alcoholism even years after sobriety. It's a lifelong battle for many of them, and there are varying degrees of victory and defeat.

Is Homosexuality Like Alcoholism?

The homosexuality and alcoholism comparisons lined up perfectly in my mind and my rhetoric for a long time. Yet, as I began to read the testimonies of gay and lesbian Christians and know some personally as friends, my analogy slowly unraveled. The breakdown was not in the two previously mentioned parallels—it was instead a point of divergence that I had never considered. In lining up the testimonies of alcoholics and of homosexuals, a glaring contrast emerged.

Alcoholics, no matter how much they labored to get sober, were always glad they had quit drinking. They knew it ultimately led to misery and that sobriety was the path to a better life, even if it would be a psychological and spiritual war they might continuously wage. This was not the same testimony I witnessed from gays and lesbians, nor witnessed by other thoughtful and otherwise conservative theologians[56].

Conversion therapy, designed to cause homosexuals to resist their romantic attractions, is littered with stories of identity problems, depression, and attempted suicide[57-58]. Nor does it have any backing in the medical community. The only study that ever suggested conversion therapy was remotely effective was published in 2003 by Dr. Robert L. Spitzer and was used in anti-gay arguments, including my own, for years following. By 2012 though, Dr. Spitzer had issued a public apology for his study. He acknowledged that it was not peer-reviewed and was methodologically flawed to the point of being medically useless[59].

Even the president of Exodus International, the leading force in the "ex-gay movement" that advocated conversion therapy for decades, in 2013 announced that conversion therapy did not work and that all the gays he had worked with still retained strong homosexual feelings—himself included[60]. A few months later, the organization shut down altogether.

Yet the ex-president of Exodus International was only one of the highest profile ex-gay movement leaders, most of who were committed Christians, who have since renounced their previous work and admitted that their so-called conversion to heterosexuality was destructive and unsustainable. Of those former ex-gay leaders, many have returned to being openly gay[61].

In this fraying contrast to alcoholism, I could not reconcile the fact that those who had been so spiritually equipped, so dedicated to overcoming their homosexuality, were being so psychologically and spiritually wrecked in the process. Escaping alcoholism, though difficult, leads to joy. Escaping from one's own sexuality seemed far too often to lead only to crushing despair.

Delivered from Homosexuality?

Yet what about that gay or lesbian of whom you may have heard, or know at your church, who claims to have left the "gay lifestyle" by the power of God's grace? Perhaps these leaders failed because they simply did not rely on God enough, and this particular gay or lesbian you have in mind is truly the shining example of genuine repentance and redemption.

First, consider that this is what many people undoubtedly said about the formerly ex-gay leaders. We should never be surprised by our fallen nature's ability to deceive ourselves and those around us. This is even more likely to happen when religious devotion or moral obligation acts as a motivating factor. Christian naiveté surrounding these testimonies is not just doctrinally self-serving, it's spiritually damaging. By so readily buying into claims of being delivered from homosexual to heterosexual orientations, we encourage the person now claiming to be straight to pretend to live, what is in all likelihood, a well-intentioned farce.

However, it is also unfair to say that all people who claim to have successfully and happily left behind their same-sex attractions are simply engaged in a tragic charade. Sexuality is always more complicated than all-or-nothing propositions. In light of this, there are some other explanations for those who genuinely claim to be "ex-gay." The most obvious of these is that they were never gay or lesbian in the first place. They may have exhibited some degree of bisexuality, and choosing to be only romantically involved only with the opposite sex, in response to religious or social pressure, was a functional trade-off[62].

The second explanation, one that requires knowing a deeper history of a person's narrative, is that his or her experience with homosexuality was so wrapped up with promiscuity or sexual abuse as to make it psychologically synonymous with homosexuality. By leaving behind the "gay lifestyle," certainly a lifestyle that often includes promiscuity, a person will experience greater happiness for abandoning the self-destructive behavior of sex outside of marriage. However, in these cases, they are unable to distinguish between their same-sex attractions and the negative effects of promiscuity or abuse. As a result, they incorrectly label their resisting same-sex attractions as liberating.

The third explanation is that their testimony is entirely valid. The Holy Spirit has altered, for whatever reason, their same-sex attractions, and they are now either maintaining celibacy comfortably or pursuing heterosexual relationships. Despite the disdain that meets these claims in more progressive secular circles, I am deeply convicted that we cannot set hard limits on the power of the Holy Spirit to make radical changes in peoples' lives, even in aspects of their sexual orientation.

Doesn't accepting these claims of changed sexual orientation imply homosexuality was wrong to begin with though? Not in the least. The complexity surrounding the causes of sexual orientation, combined with acknowledgment that a homosexual orientation inevitably will make aspects of life for an individual more difficult than if one was heterosexual, means LGBT allies need not be threatened by the rare apparent change in sexual orientation. In the very least, we must acknowledge that God does grant some people the gift and calling of celibacy.

That being said, I think it also important to acknowledge how incredibly rare these instances are. Remember that all modern medical research rejects being able to change one's sexual orientation, and that even a growing number of Christian conversion therapy organizations are admitting that they have never seen long-term transformation on that level in their own programs. Some non-inclusive Christians, however, long to hold on to those painfully few, but highly publicized stories, where someone was ironically "loved" out of engaging in same-sex relationships by Christians[63]. The non-inclusive doctrine against homosexuality must be preserved at all costs, so even a minority report of one in a million will provide sufficient psychological comfort.

There is really no argument that can be made in the face of this kind of ideological devotion, for there will always be someone homosexual enough (bisexual will suffice) and religiously motivated enough to be used as the poster child for non-inclusive agenda. Yet for those less dedicated, a handful of ex-gay or "post-gay" testimonies and a nice website will come off as an affront to reality[64].

To be fair, the most compelling case is now made by celibate gay spokespeople, such as the winsome Dr. Wesley Hill, who assert the permanence of their homosexual orientation *and* a duty of lifelong celibacy in light of it. However, even an erudite advocate like Dr. Hill acknowledges that his deepest source of doubt that same-sex romance is actually sinful comes from having so many friends "who are really passionate Christians, are deeply invested in the life of the church, are fighting for healthy celibacy, and seeing that it is leaving them in despair. They really want a joyful celibate life, and they're just not finding it."[65]

Even if we take the handful of joyfully celibate gays and lesbians at their word that they are truly both, Dr. Hill admits that they are the exception and not the rule. Without an authentic spiritual calling for celibacy, non-inclusive Christians cannot fairly hold up celibate gay spokespeople as the standard that all Christians with same-sex attractions must imitate.

The Efficacy of the Holy Spirit

There is also a theological flipside to acknowledging that some Christians may effectively resist same-sex attractions and go on to live an abundant life without internal turmoil. If those who do support same-sex relationships must acknowledge the reality of at least some of these testimonies, then those who do not support same-sex relationships must acknowledge the reality of gay and lesbian Christians experiencing a guiltless and joyful walk with God.

The testimonies from partnered gays and lesbians who tell of a happy life, whether in marriages where it is legal, or in life partnerships where it is not, are far too numerous to even begin to count. They certainly outnumber ex-gay testimonies. Again, this is something even I had to acknowledge when I was opposed to same-sex relationships. But what I was reluctant to entertain was that many of these relationships are comprised not of just two secular individuals reporting a secular kind of happiness, but of two individuals who love Jesus and report relational joy and spiritual growth. Not only that, but many tell of an assurance by the Holy Spirit that gave them peace about the relationship[66].

At first, these kinds of testimonies from Christian gays and lesbians were easy enough to write off as heretical and sinfully rationalized. They only thought God was accepting the relationship, because their perverse hearts were so willing to construct creative spiritual alibis to placate a guilty conscience. I shamelessly parroted Paul in 2 Timothy 3:5, where he describes that the most wicked of false-Christians will be found "having the appearance of godliness, but denying its power." (ESV) However, as I read or heard firsthand more and more similar stories of peace and fulfillment in prayerfully discerned same-sex relationships, I found myself at the crossroads of a choice. It was no longer a question of whether I would doubt the honesty and integrity of those I knew in same-sex relationships. It was a question of whether I would doubt the power of the Holy Spirit.

Do we truly believe that the Holy Spirit has the power to convict us of sin and affirm God-honoring paths for our lives? If so, then the growing number of gay and lesbian Christians across denominational lines who report sacredness and joy in their relationships forces us to consider the very efficacy of the Spirit. It seems as if the only means by which we can discount the testimony of people in same-sex relationships is by denying the power of the Holy Spirit to provide reliable witnesses from within the ranks of the Christians in whom God resides.

We have to ask what is more likely. Is every single Christian gay and lesbian testifying to spiritual peace about their orientation spiritually confused, if not demonically misled? Or, that at least one of them has actually received affirmation and peace from the Holy Spirit? If we acknowledge the latter, we affirm our basic orthodox teaching that is most clearly taught in Romans 8:5-6. Paul explains to us,

> *For those who live according to the flesh set their minds on the things of the flesh, but those who live according to the Spirit set their minds on the things of the Spirit. For to set the mind on the flesh is death, but to set the mind on the Spirit is life and peace. (ESV)*

Yet, if we are convinced of the former—that all open Christian gays and lesbians are either in some form of denial or spiritual confusion when they say that God has granted them peace—then we are required to do some serious theological gymnastics on the reliability of the Spirit in the lives of believers. It would be surprising, then, for non-inclusive Christians who have declared fidelity to biblical authority, in contrast to other Christians who they claim have abandoned it, to be so willing to cordon off the applicability and scope of Scripture to preserve a particular doctrine.

It is not only uncharitable, but also unbiblical, to only accept the testimony of other Christians as long as it comports with our personal doctrine. Believing in the reality of the Holy Spirit requires us to trust that the Spirit still speaks truth through the majority of believers in whom the Spirit resides. This does not mean truth that contradicts Scripture, obviously, but rather truth that clarifies the Bible's teachings and brings our theology closer to a seamless reality.

Chapter Eight

Biblical Equality, Human Rights, and History

The theological culture that makes evangelicalism in particular so wonderfully passionate with its declaration of the Gospel is in many ways the same influence that makes evangelicalism less aware of the Church's wider history. Each generation has a tendency to view itself facing unprecedented and unparalleled challenges. This ahistorical approach on the one hand gives a powerful urgency to declaring the Gospel, but on the other also provides little historical wisdom and perspective to understand our current cultural contexts. All Christians would be wise to take a note from history.

I've already mentioned that homosexuality found favor by some throughout Christendom into the 12th century. Perhaps more importantly though, we should also take notice of how the Church has handled other controversial issues during the last 200 years in America—namely, slavery, African-American civil rights, and women's rights. In all of these cases, many Christians were at the forefront of what is commonly called "the right side of history." Christians led the battle to abolish slavery. Christians organized churches to march for African-American civil rights. Christians agitated for women's suffrage and, a generation later, for women's equality.

That Christians were on the forefront of these movements is not coincidental either. Historically, since the existence of the Early Church, advances in human rights have followed wherever the Gospel has been proclaimed. Even though furthering human rights is not itself the message of the Gospel, it is an inescapable implication of our equality in Christ. The Apostle Paul declares in his letter to the Galatians:

> **For all of you who were baptized into Christ have clothed yourselves with Christ. There is neither Jew nor Greek, there is neither slave nor free man, there is neither male nor female; for you are all one in Christ Jesus. 3:27-28 (NASB)**

In an ancient culture where clothing overtly signaled one's place in society, the notion of all believers being clothed in Christ is dangerously subversive. If there was any question about its implications for equality, Paul spells it out for his audience. All people, regardless of their culture, socio-economic status, or sex, are one in Christ.

The Apostle Peter realized this as well. In the book of Acts, God reveals to him in a dream that that non-Jews, whom Peter had previously considered outside of God's grace, are equally able to participate in the Kingdom of God. When Peter meets with a group of non-Jews, he explains in Acts 10:28, "You yourselves know how unlawful it is for a man who is a Jew to associate with a foreigner or to visit him; and yet God has shown me that I should not call any man unholy or unclean." (NASB)

Still, Peter hadn't yet understood fully the radical inclusivity of the Gospel. He still waffled on the full inclusion of Gentiles into the Church. Eventually, Peter realizes that non-Jews aren't just permitted to convert to Christianity so long as they renounce their ethnicity and begin acting like Jews. This is accomplished when Paul himself confronts Peter on this religious prejudice, and ultimately convinces him that the nature of the Gospel is such that all people should be equally accepted into the Church (Galatians 2:11-16).

Nor do we find this full inclusion of previously excluded people limited to only ethnicities and cultures. In Acts 8:26-40, the Apostle Philip encounters an Ethiopian eunuch who is returning from a spiritual pilgrimage to Jerusalem. A eunuch in its ancient definition was a man who was incapable of procreation. Either because of an actual castration or having no sexual interest in women, a eunuch may have been homosexual or transgender. We have no way of knowing why this man was considered a eunuch, but we do know that his sexuality was outside the heteronormative spectrum. He was a sexual minority.

This eunuch also had a copy of the scroll from the prophet Isaiah, which contains dramatic messianic references to Jesus. Naturally then, Philip asks if he understands what he is reading, but the eunuch replies, "How can I, unless someone guides me?" Now, this is a puzzling response considering where the Ethiopian man has been. He's just visited Jerusalem. Surely, of all places, there was someone who could have taught him about Isaiah? The Jewish reader of Acts though would have instantly understood the dilemma. Why? In Deuteronomy 23:1, eunuchs are forbidden from entering the temple. This eunuch's sexuality or gender identity was keeping him from being fully included in the Lord's spiritual community.

Such a biblical prohibition, however, seems to have had no impact on Philip, who promptly jumps in his chariot and shares the Gospel with him. Without any negative mention of his eunuch identity by Philip or the narrator, the Ethiopian embraces Jesus as Lord, is immediately baptized, and returns to his home nation rejoicing. A sexual minority, excluded by ancient Judaism, was fully included by an apostle of Jesus Christ.

What does this mean for us today? As a side effect of the Gospel, we should always find our prejudices undermined and our churches challenged to be radically inclusive of all people. Next, taking a cue from the Great Commandment to love God and neighbor, Scripture must be filtered through the "Rule of Love." Lastly, and perhaps most difficult, we should be very wary of any doctrinal interpretation by privileged and powerful Christians that weighs against the marginalized and oppressed.

Though the Church has not always obeyed these ancient and orthodox principles, passages like those found in Acts and Galatians (as well as Philemon) have stoked a consistent theological fire for human rights advances down through the centuries. From resisting Roman infanticide practices to the "confessing church" that resisted the Nazis, there have always been Christians who have carried this torch.

Today, we hold up the Christians who took the implications of Gospel seriously as shining examples of those who made brave stands for equality when it wasn't popular to do so. We love stories of abolitionists, freedom riders, and women's suffragists. These are the Christians we prefer to remember, though. We should remember these bold men and women of faith, but perhaps just as much, we should also remember the Christians who fought to keep slavery, oppress African-Americans, and subjugate women in the name of boldly standing on God's Word.

Slavery

Take, for example, the many defenses of slavery by ministers in the antebellum South. Here is one argument that was advanced on the grounds that since the Bible is without any error, it would be impossible for the Bible to tolerate the moral norm of slavery at any point if it indeed were evil.

> *"...the right of holding slaves is clearly established in the Holy Scriptures, both by precept and example... Had the holding of slaves been a moral evil, it cannot be supposed that the inspired Apostles ... would have tolerated it for a moment in the Christian Church. In proving this subject justifiable by Scriptural authority, its morality is also proved; for the Divine Law never sanctions immoral actions."*
> *– Richard Furman, Baptist State Convention, Letter to South Carolina Governor, 1822*

We don't like to admit these Christians are part of the history of the Church in America. If we do acknowledge them, we tend to brush them off as horribly backward or ignorant. However, that judgment is usually made retrospectively from the more enlightened eyes of a future generation. At the time, the defenders of slavery, segregation, and sexism were actually making very sophisticated arguments. The brilliant and prolific minister of the Second Presbyterian Church in Charleston, South Carolina, the Rev. Thomas Smyth, made such a case for slavery in a sermon just after the beginning of the Civil War in 1861, concluding that,

> *"God is introduced to give dignity and emphasis ... and then He is banished. It was this very atheistic Declaration [of Independence] which had inspired the 'higher law' doctrine of the radical antislavery men. If the mischievous abolitionists had only followed the Bible instead of the godless Declaration, they would have been bound to acknowledge that human bondage was divinely ordained. The mission of southerners was therefore clear; they must defend the word of God against abolitionist infidels."*

Arguments for slavery like these were crafted by men with advanced degrees in theology and philosophy, and those Christian intellectuals were absolutely convinced their position was biblical. Yet not only did they believe their position was "divinely ordained," but the more progressive Christian view of abolition was accused of denying the authority of the Bible. Sound familiar?

Women's Suffrage and Segregation

These theological defenses of oppression did not end with the abolition of slavery, as if pro-slavery pastors were an unfortunate blot on an otherwise clean record of standing for justice. When women began to organize for the right to vote and for other basic measures of equality, they were met with similar Christian resistance. Here, the Rev. Prof. H.M. Goodwin writes a crushing condemnation of women's suffrage that would be reprinted for decades.

> *"Woman is made to be the complement and help-mate,*

not the rival of man. To the man is given physical strength, executive force, mastership, leadership—in a word, headship in the family, in the field, and in the State. Hence government is his prerogative by nature. To the woman is given a finer and more delicate organization, not inferior but different in kind and quality, fitting her as manifestly for private and domestic life, and its not less responsible duties. To deny or ignore this law is to deny the plainest facts, and to fly in the face of nature itself. Nature and reason, no less than Scripture, declares man to be the "head of the woman" and of the family, and for the same reason he is the proper head and ruler of the State...

The equality of the sexes, in the only sense in which the term can be properly used, is perfectly consistent with subordination of rank and place, as even theology teaches in the doctrine of the Trinity, where the Son is subordinate and obedient to the Father, yet one with Him in all divine attributes.

This whole movement for female suffrage, is, at least in its motive and beginning, a rebellion against the divinely ordained position and duties of woman..."[67]

Arguments like these are eerily similar to the anti-gay marriage arguments of today. One need only substitute the phrase "female suffrage" for "gay marriage," and we would have a modern anti-gay talking point.

Then for the third time in less than 150 years, an embarrassing number of Christian leaders fought to keep segregation within the United States. One notable Baptist leader, the Rev. James F. Burks of Norfolk, warned that integration was an affront to "plain truth of the word of God" and that the Supreme Court decision ending legal segregation in Brown v. Board of Education was a sign of the approaching apocalypse.

> *"Man, in overstepping the boundary lines God has drawn, has taken another step in the direction of inviting the Judgment of Almighty God. This step of racial integration is but another stepping stone toward the gross immorality and lawlessness that will be characteristic of the last days."*

However, to only note that the Bible was invoked for defenses of injustice would be to miss the point. The Bible has been hijacked to incorrectly affirm or condemn everything under the sun. What should stand out to us is that affirmations of oppression were considered by many within their generation to be defending the Word of God against those who would subvert its authority—which inevitably included "liberal" ministers and Christian activists advocating for human rights and greater equality. Though it may be hard to imagine, the moral validity of slavery and the subjugation of women were at one point considered face value, straightforward, and biblical interpretations of Scripture.

The Historical Blind Spots in Biblical Interpretation

These kinds of interpretations possessed fatal blind spots in their methodology. Again, let us briefly return to the antebellum slavery debate to understand how many Christians did, and still do, interpret Scripture.

James Henley Thornwell, a politically influential minister and theology professor, claimed that the Bible "listed over twenty separate citations from Genesis to Paul supporting Biblical acceptance of slavery" and that "the Scriptures not only fail to condemn slavery," Thornwell argued, "they as distinctly sanction it as any other social condition of man."[68]

Agreeing with this straightforward reading of the Bible, an entire body of Presbyterian ministers concluded,

> *"The holding of slaves, so far from being a sin in the sight of God, is nowhere condemned in his Holy Word—that it is in accordance with the example, or consistent with the precepts of patriarchs, prophets and apostles...Therefore, they who assume the contrary position, and lay it down as a fundamental principle in morals and religions, that all slaveholding is wrong, proceed upon false principles."*[69]

Today, we know how wrong of a biblical interpretation this was, but the reason we know is precisely because we're not reading Scripture straightforwardly. Thornwell and the pro-slavery theologians were right. At face value, the biblical witness speaks with one voice regarding slavery, and that witness clearly permits it.

The way Christians in the 18th and 19th centuries came to reject slavery then was not by stacking up the most relevant biblical verses about slavery. Such an approach would not have gotten them far. To the contrary, it reinforced the interpretation of the privileged and powerful white slave owners to justify perpetual racial slavery.

Instead, abolitionist Christians applied the wider biblical lenses of equality in Christ, the "Rule of Love," and the belief that God desires to lift up the marginalized and oppressed. Eventually, all Christians understood these wider biblical principles to overrule the straightforward reading of the Bible on the issue of slavery.

So when non-inclusive Christians today demand a face value, straightforward, and so-called biblical interpretation of Scripture as a trump card for condemning same-sex relationships, our Christian history should give us pause. This was exactly the same way of interpreting the Bible used by pro-slavery Christians. This is exactly the same interpretative blind spot plaguing us. It is all too easy to fall back on defending the "plain truth of the Word of God"—a dangerously manipulative phrase in and of itself—and pegging anyone who disagrees as promoting an overly liberal, overly academic, or overly contextualized agenda.

Such an approach fails to take into account the crucial biblical lenses of equality in Christ, the "Rule of Love," and a healthy suspicion of a doctrinal interpretation by heterosexual church leadership that weighs against homosexual people who are also effectively barred from church leadership. For any biblical issue that directly affects interpersonal relationships, this is simply an unfaithful way to read our Bibles. Yet, when we apply these three broader interpretive principles, we quickly find that this more holistic engagement with Scripture makes it increasingly difficult to justify the perpetual barring of equal rights for LGBT people in our society and churches.

Condemnation with a Smile

A frequent response to this pattern of Christians in America often placing themselves on the wrong side of history is to point out the difference in tone. The ministers that defended slavery, women's inequality, and segregation were guided by hate—at least, that's one explanation. Non-inclusive pastors today who declare any expression of homosexuality a sin are not saying this in hate, but in love. In fact, they seem to go out of their way whenever they talk about the issue, to mention loving LGBT people out of their sin. Surely, then, this means we've bucked the pattern of history.

The gentle fashion in which many non-inclusive pastors are now talking about homosexuality is certainly preferable to fiery sermons preaching damnation on gays and lesbians. Yet this softer tone can clearly be seen as an evolution of non-inclusive Christian rhetoric. As the gay rights culture went mainstream in the 1990s and Christians began to actually know gays and lesbians as neighbors, co-workers and relatives, straightforward condemnation had lost its viability as an effective rhetorical tool. Whether Christians said it openly or not, the evangelical movement suddenly felt a lot less certain that same-sex relationships were sinful. Having a son or daughter "come out" will do that. As a result, evangelical pastors wisely responded with a softer, more upbeat argument against LGBT people. But condemnation with a smile is not without its historical precedent either.

During the Civil Rights Era of the 1960s, the founder of Bob Jones University in Greenville, South Carolina, gave an exhaustive 32-page sermon on Easter. This sermon explained why the Bible supported segregation and why it was patently unbiblical to "mix races." Like any good pastor, he begins with an appeal to relying on obedience to the clear teachings of Scripture.

> *"Now, we folks at Bob Jones University believe that whatever the Bible says is so; and we believe it says certain fundamental things that all Bible-believing Christians accept; but when the Bible speaks clearly about any subject, that settles it. Men do not always agree, because some are dumb—some people are spiritually dumb; but when the Bible is clear, there is not any reason why everybody should not accept it." (p. 1)*

After establishing his fidelity to the Bible, Rev. Jones transitions to a part of the Bible that seemingly makes it abundantly clear that races were meant to exist separately.

> *"Now, notice—this is an important verse—the twenty-sixth verse of the seventeenth chapter of the Acts of the Apostles, 'And hath made of one blood all nations*

of men for to dwell on all the face of the earth.' But do not stop there, '...and hath determined the times before appointed, and the bounds of their habitation.' Now, what does that say? That God Almighty fixed the bounds of their habitations. That is as clear as anything that was ever said." (p. 6)

But Rev. Jones wants his listeners to know that he's not a racist. The Bible, in his interpretation, is against racism.

"You talk about a superior race and an inferior race and all that kind of situation. Wait a minute. No race is inferior to the will of God. Get that clear. If a race is in the will of God, it is not inferior. It is a superior race. You cannot be superior to another race if your race is in the will of God and the other race is in the will of God. But the purposes of these races were established by Almighty God; and when man attempts to run contrary to the directive will of God for this world, there is trouble." (p. 8)

In fact, Rev. Jones expresses hurt and frustration that some people can't understand that he is simply standing for the clear teaching of Scripture, and is in no way acting out of hatred or bitterness.

"A Christian relationship does not mean a marriage relationship. You can be a Christian and have fellowship with people that you would not marry and that God does not want you to marry and that if you should marry you would be marrying outside the will of God. Why can't you see that? Why can't good, solid, substantial people who do not have any hatred and do

not have any bitterness see that? Let's approach this thing in a Christian way." (p. 28)

Sermons like these fail to make the history books because it was neither scathingly conservative nor revolutionarily progressive for its time. Within the entirety of the sermon, Rev. Jones goes out of his way to affirm the equality of African-Americans, even tritely complimenting them, while steadfastly justifying segregation as a biblical edict. Parts of Scripture were effective in undermining this preacher's most racist dispositions, but he could not—for the sake of the Word of God—abandon his commitment to segregation and his condemnation of the civil rights movement that was sweeping the American South.

We as Christians are still rightfully embarrassed by the smiling segregationist pastors of the past. Smiling pastors who gently rebuke same-sex relationships today should not then provide us false assurance that we are somehow avoiding the same mistake American Christianity has made on major human rights issues three other times in the last two centuries.

The Right Side of History?

This is, of course, not a deductive argument, but an inductive argument. It might be entirely possible that American Christianity got it wrong many times in the past about human rights, but this time about gay rights may be different. Oddly enough, the president from Bob Jones made a similar statement elsewhere in his sermon where he acknowledged many Christians were wrong to defend slavery, but were now right to defend segregation. Irony aside though, even progressive Christians should acknowledge that as supporters of same-sex relationships, we just might have been duped by a degenerate secular culture. Perhaps we've just fallen prey to the "spirit of the age" hinted at in Ephesians 2:2, now deceptively baptized in civil rights lingo and claims of being on the "right side of history."

After all, didn't a large part of progressive secular academia at the turn of 20th century predict that restricted immigration and forced sterilization would eventually eliminate "inferior" races and those deemed regressive? Didn't the Soviet premiere, Nikita Khrushchev, quite presumptively declare to Western ambassadors, "Whether you like it or not, history is on our side. We will bury you"? Certainly, merely claiming to be on the right side of history doesn't make it so.

Yet note the fundamental difference when the inevitably of history has been invoked incorrectly. The right side of history has always been on the side of treating human beings with more rights and more dignity. The failed claims have sought to allow human beings fewer rights and grant less dignity. Eugenics and communism may have failed for a number of reasons, but this reason alone was sufficient for forfeiting their supposed historical inevitability.

We cannot faithfully escape from the arc of

history with an appeal to historical nihilism either, as if the world can only get worse. Christianity is a uniquely historical religion that embraces linear, purposive history. God is sovereign over the world's history and he promised that his Kingdom, in spite of difficulties, would advance within that history. Therefore, history is not a random smattering of progress and regress, nor can the gates of hell prevail indefinitely against God's Kingdom. Certainly, since the breaking in of the new reign of God at the incarnation of Christ, human society ever since has inched forward in a redemptive sense.

Pointing out the hubris of movements that worked against human rights and dignity correctly acknowledges that the right side of history cannot be manufactured. God, the author of history, guides his enduring truth over any fleeting spirit of the age. Accusations of naivety against gay rights supporters, however, completely lack the historical tether to abandoned movements like eugenics and communism. Granting equal rights and dignity to LGBT people fits an objective pattern of moving forward on the right side of both secular and Christian history.

There is one other historical factor, though, that indicates that this sort of skepticism by non-inclusive Christians is probably without prophetic merit. The public opinion polls that follow LGBT rights and the normalization of same-sex relationships strongly indicate we are dealing with a human rights issue and not a conventional moral issue. For example, look at public opinion polls since 1973's Roe v. Wade decision regarding whether abortion should be illegal. What you'll find is gradually fluctuating numbers that at some points indicate a majority of American culture supportive of abortion rights and at other times a majority more supportive of the rights of the fetus.

Had abortion rights truly been a landmark human rights issue on par with the abolition of slavery or the right for women to vote, 1973 should have been the year public opinion reflected the least support for abortion rights. Following that, there would have been a steady progression of support that would have culminated, essentially, in complete cultural acceptance. After all, even 50 years following the African-American civil rights era, hardly anyone would even consider interracial marriage immoral. A steady progression of cultural acceptance of abortion rights has never happened though. It is still one of the more controversial ethical issues of our day, and unlike with previous civil rights issues, no consensus appears to be in sight for American society.

LGBT rights, however, bears no resemblance to abortion rights when comparing the public opinion. As I mentioned earlier, since 1996 support for marriage equality and same-sex relationships has been growing at a rate of at least 1 to 2 percent each year[70]. With only one minor and brief reversal in 2003, acceptance of gays and lesbians in society is progressing almost identically to the other major human and civil rights shifts in American history. If anything, it is faster.

So is it possible that non-inclusive Christians, in rejecting the moral legitimacy of same-sex relationships, are somehow *not* standing in the way of human rights? It is indeed *possible*. But given the direction of the historical evidence, it seems very *unlikely*. And while it is fair to ask questions about our post-Enlightenment context, cynically writing this off as a modern elitist Western trend only buys oneself enough time to grow old and die without having to worry about feeling morally backward.

We cannot brush off what should be a haunting observation, that the progress of gay rights and the cultural acceptance of same-sex relationships mirror previous human and civil rights movements in the United States.

Moreover, each of these movements not only encompassed a legal component, but a social and ethical dimension as well. Eventually, all of these rights embedded themselves as moral goods within society. Few Americans today merely "tolerate" women in the workplace or interracial relationships, only to personally believe it's immoral. We have come to see these expressions of social diversity as signs of an ethical and flourishing society. There is little reason to imagine same-sex relationships will be viewed any differently a generation from now.

If most American churches fail to recognize this pattern within the next ten years, the damage to the reputation of Christianity will not be measured in years, but in decades. The advance of the Gospel will be halted much in the same way when churches in former dictatorships were discredited when Christians failed, by-and-large, to resist the oppressive rule of the regime. Christianity remained in those nations after the dictator's fall, but it lost its moral authority and the power to persuade the people that the Gospel is truly "good news."

Our challenge as Christians in the United States is that the Gospel should always be associated with the good news of human rights and equality, not prejudice and oppression. The natural implications of the Gospel should challenge Christians to be on the cutting edge of human rights movements, or, at the very least, to not oppose them. The way we respond to LGBT rights, viewing it either as a human rights issue or as a destructive sin issue, will be a determining factor in just how good the Good News of Jesus Christ will seem to the next generation.

Chapter Nine

Our *Imago Dei* and a Moral Objection to the Gospel

The last theological argument we should examine briefly is perhaps more novel than most, and also the most complex. It is rooted in our Christian belief that we are made in the *imago Dei*, or "image of God." In Paul's teaching in Romans 2:14-16, he explains,

> *For when Gentiles, who do not have the law, by nature do what the law requires, they are a law to themselves, even though they do not have the law. They show that the work of the law is written on their hearts, while their conscience also bears witness, and their conflicting*

> ***thoughts accuse or even excuse them on that day when, according to my gospel, God judges the secrets of men by Christ Jesus. (ESV)***

Though we are fallen and inherently sinful, we still retain the *imago Dei* and the moral conscience that comes with being made in God's image. Our total depravity does affect every part of our being, but it does not make every part of our being totally depraved. According to the Bible, we are still capable of determining right from wrong, albeit imperfectly (1 Corinthians 8:7). The ability to make moral decisions is by no means limited to Christians, but is granted to all people, which is a natural consequence of what the Reformer Jean Calvin called "common grace."

It logically follows then that it is important for Christians to perform serious self-reflection when non-Christians reject the Gospel on moral grounds.

There are three general categories in which I've found that people reject the Gospel: evidentiary objections, emotional objections and moral objections. Evidential objections claim that there is not sufficient evidence to believe that the Bible is historically reliable and that Jesus is the savior of humanity. Emotional objections come from a person who is unwilling to submit his or her life to God's control, either out of a lack of trust in God's goodness or a greater desire to continue sinning. Moral objections emerge from a belief that something about the teachings of the Bible or Christianity is actually immoral.

Moral objections may surprise some of us since we have been conditioned to believe religion is innately "moral," if not moralistic, and the absence of religion is innately immoral. Yet consider a religion outside of Christianity. Many people in the West, Christian and non-Christian alike, reject Islam not because they find the evidence lacking that Muhammad was Allah's final prophet. Few Westerners will research Islam even to that extent. Islam is rejected in the West because most people in our society perceive the teachings of Islam to be immoral in nature. We view it as oppressive of women, intolerant of other religions and strict to the point of causing psychological repression.

Two Moral Objections to the Gospel

It shouldn't surprise Christians then, that people might reject the Gospel on some kind of moral ground as well. In my experience ministering to young adults, I've witnessed an astonishingly consistent pattern in what these moral objections to Christianity are. Surprisingly, I have never met someone from the millennial generation (those born between the early 1980s and 2000) who rejects the Bible's teaching on sexual purity and fidelity. Some have struggled with it, but it is not used as a reason to refuse Christ's forgiveness. The two moral objections to Christianity—without exception—since I began ministering to students on a liberal arts campus have been the salvific exclusivity of Christ and the condemnation of same-sex relationships.

The moral objection to the salvific exclusivity of Christ, the doctrine that people can only enter into Heaven through Jesus' atoning sacrifice on the cross, stems from an accusation of unfairness. Again, in my experience, this objection consistently comes from a misconception of what the doctrine of exclusivity of Christ actually means, or from a faulty assumption about the inherent goodness and worthiness of humans.

As disappointing as it is to discover that American Christianity has done a poor job of teaching why salvation can only come through Jesus, on another level we should be hopeful for the person who genuinely rejects the Gospel on moral grounds. He or she is making a moral stand out of a particular belief in God's goodness and a genuine understanding of justice, a moral virtue that exists specifically because he or she is made in the *imago Dei*.

If a moral objection can be primarily a matter of misperception, then this may very well be preferable for the individual in question. Why would we want someone to believe in the Gospel out of self-interest (acquiring salvation) and in appeasing an unjust God who unfairly sends other less fortunate souls to Hell? Although there may be a rare exception, any authentic and rational moral objection to a religion strongly indicates it either to be a misunderstanding of a doctrine or a valid critique of a doctrine.

Therefore, when young adults continuously tell me they are skeptical of Christianity on the basis of its condemnation of same-sex relationships, we need to consider what is really happening. They are not directly rejecting the historicity of Jesus, his claims of divinity, or even the authority of the Bible. Few are so familiar with the Bible as to know specifically where the Bible might condemn same-sex relationships. Most non-Christians, and even many Christians, only understand this as a doctrine of Christianity.

Our Moral Compass and the *Imago Dei*

More importantly, unlike with recreational drug use or premarital sex, this is not an objection to Christianity out of desires to gratify sinful behavior. In fact, of all the potential sins one might be tempted to commit, homosexuality for heterosexual people is rarely one of them. So being skeptical of Christianity out of a perception that Christianity teaches that all homosexual behavior is sinful is unequivocally a moral objection. Some might contest that this is a culturally induced objection, but if so, it would be no more induced than that of Western person's moral objection to Islam over its attitudes toward women. In standing against a perceived injustice towards gay and lesbian people, these non-Christians are counter-intuitively resisting God because they are obeying the moral compass that God created in them.

This is akin to the literary example found in the work of Mark Twain, who masterfully reenacts a heroic moral objection to religion in *The Adventures of Huckleberry Finn*. Huck Finn, who has befriended a runaway slave named Jim, recalls from Sunday school how great a sin it is to help slaves escape their rightful masters. *"People that acts as I'd been acting about [Jim],"* he'd been told, *"goes to everlasting fire."* The young Huck understandably wants to clear the conscience that has programmed him to feel like he has sinned. So he begins writing a letter to the owner, Miss Watson, to tell her where to find Jim.

> *I felt good and all washed clean of sin for the first time I had ever felt so in my life, and I knowed I could pray now. But I didn't do it straight off, but laid the paper down and set there thinking—thinking how good it was all this happened so, and how near I come to being lost and going to hell.*

> *And went on thinking. And got to thinking over our trip down the river; and I see Jim before me, all the time; in the day, and in the night-time, sometimes moonlight, sometimes storms, and we a floating along, talking, and singing, and laughing. But somehow I couldn't seem to strike no places to harden me against him, but only the other kind.*

> *I'd see him standing my watch on top of his'n, stead of calling me, so I could go on sleeping; and see him how glad he was when I come back out of the fog; and when I come to him agin in the swamp, up there where the feud was; and such-like times; and would always call me honey, and pet me, and do everything he could think of for me, and how good he always was; and at last I struck the time I saved him by telling the men we had smallpox aboard, and he was so grateful, and said I was the best friend old Jim ever had in the world, and*

> *the only one he's got now; and then I happened to look around, and see that paper.*
>
> *It was a close place. I took it up, and held it in my hand. I was a trembling, because I'd got to decide, forever, betwixt two things, and I knowed it. I studied a minute, sort of holding my breath, and then says to myself: "All right, then, I'll go to hell"—and tore it up.*

Was it possible, then, that Huck Finn's sense of justice was so skewed as to cause him to feel morally convicted, even in the face of the punishment of hell, that his church's moral teaching was itself immoral? Yes, but it was very unlikely, and Twain's insight and our hindsight applaud a character like Huck. However, that sense of injustice being correct was not simply because the issue in question was slavery. There was no moral clarity in Huck's worldview that slavery was wrong; rather, it was just the opposite. The reason Huck could rationally abandon his church's teachings and brave damnation was that there are few times when someone acquires a deep sense of injustice about an issue, only to be completely wrong.

While the means by which justice can be enacted is fraught with moral peril and complexity, the initial conviction that violates one's sense of justice is shockingly correct. Unlike our conceptions of right and wrong behavior, which can vary wildly even in Christianity, our collective and individual sense of injustice is incredibly cross-cultural. This part of our damaged *imago Dei* remains intact. Though it is true that injustice may go unnoticed or ignored for a long time—as was the case with American slavery—once injustice is recognized, cultures do not revert back to viewing that injustice as just.

This idea of an intuitive sense of fairness being able to cut through religions and philosophies is widely established in Christianity. It stretches from Jesus using the parable of the Good Samaritan to Socratically debating the religious lawyer on what it means to love one's neighbor. C.S. Lewis used the concept as a central apologetic tactic in proving the existence of universal truths[71]. A skeptic may say he does not believe in injustice, Lewis would say, until you steal his wallet. When we experience injustice firsthand, we acknowledge its existence, even if our philosophical beliefs don't.

Granted, even if the vast majority of young adults' (70% in 2013[72]) find that their sense of justice is violated by the doctrine that all same-sex relationships are sinful at best and perversely wicked at worst, it is still possible that their sense of justice may be wrong. However, is it likely? If it is indeed wrong, and same-sex relationships are in reality sinful, it will be the first time a culture mistakenly perceived an injustice in Western history. We need to let the sheer historical uniqueness of that statement sink in. Non-inclusive Christians are betting on the emergence of an unprecedented and tragic moment in history to vindicate their condemnation of same-sex relationships. Even the vastly influential "sexual revolution" of the 1960s, a mixed bag of progress and various excesses, never experienced anything close to this level of emerging cultural consensus about injustice.

It shouldn't provide much comfort either to blame secular media. We cannot attribute this massive sentiment of injustice to a media brainwashing. Even a majority of Millennial generation Christians (51% in 2013[73]), raised in conservative evangelical churches, are rejecting the non-inclusive doctrine on homosexuality, while retaining a commitment to what is otherwise an evangelical Christian paradigm.

Based, then, on a biblical understanding of our *imago Dei* and the sense of justice God has instilled in both Christians and non-Christians, it would seem far more likely that this moral objection to Christianity, because of the non-inclusive doctrine on homosexuality, is an accurate indictment on the injustice of the doctrine. This moral objection, rather than an intellectual or emotional objection, is a key clue in helping us discern that Christianity should not categorize same-sex relationships as a sin.

If we as Christians are serious about the integrity of our ancient belief that all people are made in the image of God and reflect moral awareness, then once again we find ourselves at an impasse. We cannot reject the moral critique of a doctrine that condemns same-sex behavior without simultaneously rejecting a coherent doctrine about the *imago Dei*. Which, then, is more precious to you?

Chapter Ten

Reformation for the Sake of the Gospel

Sometimes it's hard for me to remember that reading books like these did very little to persuade me when I was almost certain that same-sex relationships were in open rebellion to God's creative order and design. There is a hope, perhaps terribly naïve, that truth, effectively communicated, is capable of creating shifts in worldviews. This may even be true on unique occasions, but knowing full well my own stubbornness, it seems to me that worldview questions are rarely settled via the mind.

That probably sounds counter-intuitive given the evangelical emphasis on apologetics, but I believe that the intellect is only the middle of the three barriers an idea must break through in order to be internalized. If there is to be reformation in Christianity on behalf of LGBT people and for the sake of the Gospel, then worldviews will have to change through a process of new experiences, engaging the intellect, and confirmation by the Holy Spirit.

How Worldviews Change

The first cracks in a worldview often come when our experiences do not measure up to the expectations our beliefs create. For example, if I believed that all faithful Christians will be blessed financially by God, my first significant doubt to this belief probably would not come from someone pointing out countervailing biblical passages. I already "know" what I believe, and I "know" how the Bible proves my belief. Rather, the first crack would occur as I came to know at least one faithful Christian who had experienced continuous financial hardships or poverty. Visceral, tangible and immediate contradictions to the expectations of our beliefs allow for doubts.

Many of the people reading this book will be unable to genuinely consider its reasoning unless they have first undergone a contradiction of experience and belief regarding homosexuality. They are simply too willing to perform whatever theological gymnastics necessary to maintain some form of the non-inclusive position. Until someone knows at least a handful of gays and lesbians who contradict the various belief-induced expectations non-inclusive Christians possess, it will be difficult to consider anything else. Until the concrete interferes with the abstract, our worldview prefers to take refuge in the abstract.

Yet once this does happen with great enough frequency—some of us are more dedicated to our abstract worldviews than others—then we are able to consider the actual rational arguments that may shift our thinking. That is where this book, and many other lengthier and more scholarly works come into the process of worldview change. From here, people may find themselves persuaded by all or only a few arguments. Very rarely do any arguments fail to persuade, especially from well-reasoned doctrinal theories. The question is whether enough reasons and evidence were effectively advanced to create a tipping point in the mind.

This is not a tipping point to complete persuasion, mind you. The tipping point is that second in one's mind where the other belief, if but even for a lengthy moment, seems entirely possible. The 19th century American philosopher William James famously called this a "living option."[74] My prayers are that many of you, either by route of reason, the Holy Spirit, or both, find yourselves after this book thinking that it may be possible for same-sex relationships to be God-honoring relationships.

That Pesky Holy Spirit

Yet there is still a considerable leap from possible

to probable, and further still to the very likely or whatever approaches near certainty. This is the kind of leap that causes one to make a stand for a belief that will cost money, relationships and a "good" reputation in the Christian community. For a few, this last step may be almost entirely a question of intellect, but I am convinced that a newly internalized belief for most Christians emerges from a confirmation from the Holy Spirit.

When I began to come out of the theological closet with my newfound support for LGBT people, the response from some non-inclusive evangelical pastors was less than enthusiastic. Of course, they encouraged me to pray so that God could convict me of my waywardness. So in submission to the relational authority they had over me, I did. After one particularly hard meeting, I prayed to God to correct me through a personal messenger if I was indeed blessing what was actually sin. Though I also prayed that this messenger could also affirm my new position, I literally begged for a rebuke from the Spirit. My life would have been so much easier, if that would have been what happened next.

But it didn't.

Within an hour of that prayer, one of the most conservative and wise Christians I knew confessed to me—without any idea of what I had just prayed about—that she had begun to be persuaded by the Holy Spirit and her study of Scripture that homosexuality was not a sin. I sat there speechless, holding back tears. It would have been hard to imagine a more surprising messenger, sent not to rebuke me, but to confirm the convictions I believed God had been laying on my heart and mind. In fact, from this point on, every time I found myself tempted to doubt God's leading behind my reluctant reversal over homosexuality, I always found myself supplied with powerful and unexpected encouragement.

You may not experience such a clear answer to prayer, but beyond reason and evidence, you will need the Holy Spirit to confirm in your heart what you may be considering in your mind. This is why the mind is only the middle barrier to a changed worldview. Consider the highly educated Pharisee Nicodemus, who out of genuine curiosity meets with Jesus at night, but does not comprehend what Jesus is trying to teach him. Jesus answers him in John 3:10-11,

> *"Are you the teacher of Israel and yet you do not understand these things? Truly, truly, I say to you, we speak of what we know, and bear witness to what we have seen, but you do not receive our testimony." (ESV)*

Given the controversy within evangelical and conservative Christian circles, when it comes to deciding whether same-sex relationships can be God-honoring relationships, we must ultimately find an assurance that can only be provided by God. Bible study and reason alone will not be sufficient for most of us. If what has been said on these pages has drawn you into a new understanding of what God teaches through

Scripture, please pray that the Spirit would grow a peace in your heart that would match the growing evidence that affirms same-sex relationships. That kind of assurance will allow Christians to take the difficult stands necessary to advocate on behalf of LGBT people who are in desperate need of acceptance in the Christian community.

Advocacy without Quitting Your Day Job

What would this advocacy look like? For starters, it probably would not look like leaving your non-inclusive church for one that does fully include same-sex couples. I cannot emphasize enough how important showing grace is when advocating on behalf of LGBT people. Many Christians, especially many pastors, will view you as "blessing sin" and "rejecting God's Word" should you come out of the theological closet.

Some non-inclusive Christians will respectfully disagree with you, and believe it or not, these Christians are your allies. "Whoever is not against us is for us," says Jesus (Mark 9:40), so these non-inclusive Christians who respond in Christian unity deserve loving patience. Even if they remain entirely unconvinced that same-sex relationships can be spiritually healthy, their willingness to keep their sights on our overriding mission in the Gospel is commendable.

Acknowledging our current minority status within Christianity, we must be all the more committed to obeying Paul's teaching in

Ephesians 4:1-6, when he implores his fellow believers:

> *I therefore, a prisoner for the Lord, urge you to walk in a manner worthy of the calling to which you have been called, with all humility and gentleness, with patience, bearing with one another in love, eager to maintain the unity of the Spirit in the bond of peace. There is one body and one Spirit—just as you were called to the one hope that belongs to your call—one Lord, one faith, one baptism, one God and Father of all, who is over all and through all and in all. (ESV)*

However, the majority of non-inclusive Christians will often invent ways around God's command of Gospel-unity when their doctrinal idols are not appeased, and accepting same-sex relationships is all too often one such offense. Ephesians 4 will be quickly tossed aside, and any kind affirmation of same-sex relationships will be grounds for breaking ministry and fellowship. Disappointment and anger will likely be your first emotions, but we cannot respond with the same kind of self-righteousness that God may be calling us to endure. To show grace, unmerited kindness and compassion to those Christians who persecute you in God's name, may very well be the kind of obedience to Jesus that softens hearts.

We must do our best to work within our existing non-inclusive Christian communities and circles of influence as a movement of reform. This has already begun through programs like the Reformation Project, the brainchild of a Harvard-educated and gay Christian from rural Kansas,

Matthew Vines. In 2013, Vines began hosting "Bible boot camps" to equip inclusive evangelical Christians to begin challenging their own congregations about their misinterpretation of the Bible.

So if you're a Christian in leadership at a non-inclusive church, consider organizing Bible studies about homosexuality, this time with a more informed and balanced approach. Offer your support the next time a LGBT person comes to you for spiritual guidance about their orientation or relationships. It may even start with just openly acknowledging that orthodox Christians can faithfully disagree about homosexuality. There are plenty of steps you can take to stay true to your convictions that will not get you fired (at least, not immediately).

For the member of a non-inclusive church, your role is no less important. Set up a meeting with your pastor or pastors, explain why your support of same-sex relationships is biblical and humbly begin a dialogue that will encourage them to reconsider the non-inclusive doctrine. Gently correct homophobic remarks by fellow members in your church. Stand up for LGBT people who come out to the church and are removed from serving in the church. This happens more than one might think. Larger churches are very proficient at quietly asking LGBT people who officially come out to step down from whatever role in which they're serving—without the majority of the congregation ever knowing otherwise. Because of this, our LGBT brothers and sisters need spiritual allies. Without becoming full-time activists, we can all do our part to challenge our own churches to reevaluate their stances on homosexuality.

Eight Questions Every Christian Must Answer

What if though you still feel far from persuaded that same-sex relationships can be morally edifying? First it's important you ask yourself what would be necessary to persuade you. Second, you should also be comfortable responding in confidence to the questions from Christian LGBT advocates. Take a look below at eight of the most crucial points made in this book.

1) Jesus teaches in Matthew 12:7, Matthew 7:17-20 and Mark 3:4 that biblical morality should be determined by what is merciful, good and restorative and that it should not cause unnecessary sacrifice or suffering. The "Great Commandment" implies that all doctrine should conform to the "Rule of Love." Assuming we acknowledge the overwhelming evidence that changing one's sexual orientation is extremely rare, how then is demanding mandatory lifelong celibacy for gays and lesbians obedient to that teaching? How is this loving our neighbor?

2) God says in Genesis 2:18, before the creation of Eve, God describes Adam's life of forced singleness as "not good." Paul tells us in 1 Corinthians 3:9 regarding single people and celibacy, "But if they cannot exercise self-control,

they should marry. For it is better to marry than to burn with passion." How, then, is demanding mandatory lifelong celibacy for gays and lesbians honoring God's foundational decree and Paul's practical charge?

3) The Bible shows from passages like those in Deuteronomy 30:15, Isaiah 59:2, 1 John 1:6 and Romans 6:23 that all sin causes harm. According to the Bible, there is no such thing as a harmless sin. What spiritual, psychological or relational harm do same-sex marriage cause? Is there valid evidence documenting this?

4) The Bible tells us in 1 Corinthians 13:4-8,13 the attributes of what defines genuine love between people (while originally about "charitable" love, Christians have long applied it to marriage) If a same-sex marriage could meet all the rigorous standards set by Scripture for what defines this kind of love, would it still be a sin? If so, can you think of any other sin that functions like this?

5) The Bible contrasts in Galatians 5:16-23 the incompatibility of sinful behavior with the "fruit of the Spirit," that is, what a life looks like when it is led by God. This passage even makes it abundantly clear that Christians should not label anything sin if it bears the fruit of the Spirit ("against such things there is no law."). How, then, can it be explained biblically that there are gay and lesbian Christians exhibiting all the fruit of the Spirit if they're allegedly engaging in pervasive, unrepentant sin at the same time?

6) The Bible explains in 1 John 2:27 that the Holy Spirit teaches truth through the body of believers, and Romans 8:5-6 teaches particularly that the Spirit grants "life and peace" where the Spirit resides. In light of this, how can every Christian who expresses spiritual peace about being in a same-sex relationship be deluded into thinking that the peace is from the Holy Spirit?

7) The Gospel has been a historical source of inspiration for human rights, the inclusion of social "outsiders," and a threat to those with privilege and power. Can you name a time when any nation embraced a civil or human rights movement, only to recant that movement in the future? If so, how is the LGBT civil/human rights movement similar? If not, how can it be the sole exception in human history?

8) An implication of biblical doctrine of the *imago Dei* is that while cultures have always struggled to identify justice, they do correctly identify injustice. Can you name a time when any culture collectively recognized an injustice within itself, only to decide that it was actually just in the future? If so, how is the moral critique and sense of injustice from the growing majority of heterosexuals in our culture about the non-inclusive position on homosexuality similar? If not, how can it be the sole exception in human history and how would it not undermine the doctrine of the *imago Dei?*

If you find answering these questions to be both biblically and logically difficult, you're in good company with a rapidly expanding number of Christians who don't know if they can affirm same-sex relationships, but aren't sure they can condemn them either. Is the Church at a hopeless impasse then?

Forging a Truce

Pastors on both sides of this question have said that the divergent theology on homosexuality will inevitably split churches and denominations. Non-inclusive hardliners will view their position as a non-negotiable cause for biblically mandated morality, and will be unable to tolerate those who they perceive as condoning serious sin. Inclusive hardliners will view their position as a non-negotiable cause for biblically mandated equality, and will be unable to tolerate those who they perceive as condoning oppression. If this is true, deep and irreconcilable conflict will be the inevitable result.

While the Baby Boomers and Generation Xers seem to have indeed fallen into this kind of schism, I have viewed first hand the Millennial generation showing signs of forging a truce over homosexuality in their churches. Theology over same-sex relationships appears to be moving into a compartmentalized secondary tier of doctrines, much in the same way this generation already views the role of women in ministry. Millennials may personally believe women should or should not lead and teach over men, carrying similar echoes of the equality versus biblical morality debate, but the vast majority is willing to attend

Reformation for the Sake of the Gospel 151

churches of either theological position.

They are more interested in a church that proclaims the Gospel articulately and practices it winsomely than a church's position on any particular non-salvific doctrine. Over the next twenty years, the issue of openly LGBT people in evangelical churches may be very well be viewed in the same vein.

Yet, if this sort of truce seems merely more of a retreat from biblical truth for the sake tolerance than an actual Gospel-centered compromise, consider the 19th and 20th century precedent set by missionaries to Africa in dealing with polygamy. Early on, missionaries commanded converts who had multiple wives to divorce all but one wife. Not surprisingly, this lead to a plethora of social problems and relational suffering, not to mention an ironic cultural association of divorce with Christianity.

Eventually, missionaries realized that it was more faithful to the Gospel to teach the men who practiced polygamy how to love all his wives sacrificially than to divorce them in the name of an unyielding ethic of biblical morality. The result was that in the long-term, many in the next generation of indigenous Christians would organically abandon polygamy for monogamy[75].

What if non-inclusive churches could apply this principal to same-sex relationships? If you still are unable to accept any expression of homosexuality as moral, consider what it would be like to fully welcome gay and lesbian people into the life of your church without any formal endorsement of same-sex relationships. What would this look like? Treating your homosexual and bisexual congregants the same as your heterosexual congregants. You would not need to approve of their relationships, but nor would you command them to divorce themselves from the relationships they may or may not be pursuing. They would possess ecclesial equality, allowed equal access to serve and lead where they felt called by God.

Except, like how missionaries to Africa gradually phased out polygamy by effectively internalizing the implications of the Gospel within fully welcomed converts, you would not rush the timing of the Holy Spirit. If the non-inclusive doctrine against same-sex relationships is true, then one need only trust that God will eventually convict those Christians with same-sex orientations in your church to voluntarily abstain from homosexual intimacy.

This is a truce that can satisfy both non-inclusive and inclusive Christians. Non-inclusive Christians are not required to compromise their consciences, but only to rely on the orthodox belief that the Holy Spirit and holistic biblical teaching will bring any maturing believer to a conviction about sin. Inclusive Christians will get to see full ecclesial equality and inclusion extended to LGBT people, while also acknowledging that if same-sex relationships are actually sinful, the Holy Spirit will not relent in stirring conviction, confession, and repentance for those who are engaged in them. In short, where faithful Christians disagree, we agree to let God be the faithful and active arbiter, disciplining those He loves (Hebrews 12:6-11).

Would this satisfy the hardliners on either side who demand celibacy for gays and lesbians or celebration of same-sex unions? No. Yet truces are not for those who still eager to wage conflict at the cost of relationships. Truces are for those who are convinced that the toll of a conflict have become unbearably high, and despite our differences, we must now resolve those differences by a less destructive means.

The Courage to Come Off the Fence

Even still, perhaps the most important kind of reader has yet to be addressed here. There will be a temptation for many Christians, who believe it may be possible that same-sex relationships could be moral, to not actually come off the proverbial fence. Realizing the potential consequences of doing so, they may instinctively want to avoid coming to a level of confidence that would put them at odds with the non-inclusive doctrine. Sitting on the fence is much safer, since it allows one to neither condemn LGBT people nor defend them. Our consciences can rest a little easier without suffering the judgment of non-inclusive Christians, who often feel as if any evangelical who supports same-sex relationships is a traitor to evangelicalism[76].

I confess I tried to balance on the fence for years, since I feared the repercussions of finally becoming convicted that the non-inclusive doctrine on homosexuality was unbiblical. I knew if that were to happen, I would no longer be faced with a question of theology, but a question of integrity. Only cowards fail to speak up on behalf of those they themselves believe are unjustly condemned and marginalized. In some ways, I knew that could be just as tragic of a failure as the condemnations itself.

I implore you, then, not to seek the safety of sitting on the fence. For the sake of the Gospel, we do not have that luxury. We are running out of time. The polarization of society and the Church over same-sex marriage is driving much of the evangelical movement not to reconsider the non-inclusive doctrine on homosexuality, but to double down on it. Instead of repenting of this golden calf doctrine, we are claiming modern martyrdom for it.

So as secular society and mainline Christianity accept same-sex marriage as a legitimate expression of love, the ex-gay movement publicly repents of its hurtful work, and the number of open and spiritually devoted LGBT Christians grows, non-inclusive Christianity will find itself melting down more and more of its theological gold for the sake of a golden calf doctrine of condemning same-sex relationships.

If this pattern is not reversed soon, non-inclusive Christians will likely suffer the same punishment as the Hebrews experienced in the Sinai desert. Our golden calf will be melted down by God's refining fire of truth, turned to powder on the ash heap of history, and we will be forced by the larger culture to swallow it in shame and humiliation.

And the Gospel will suffer for it.

If you love the Gospel of Jesus Christ, please do not sit on the sidelines of history hoping to skirt the difficult decisions that may draw the ire of non-inclusive Christian leaders. The Gospel is of far more value than our social comfort and reputation.

Every reformation within the Church, every Christian movement that we look back on with pride, came from a faithful minority within the Church that boldly followed the teachings of Jesus. To be faithful to the implications of the Gospel will, at all points in history, lead us into a so-called heresy somewhere. From Martin Luther to Martin Luther King, Jr., to countless other Christian reformers and activists, they were all labeled heretics by the self-appointed theological gatekeepers of their day. But the heresy charge is only temporary. If we have obediently discerned the will of God, that heresy will one day become orthodoxy.

The cause of LGBT people is our generation's turning point in history, the moment where God again is calling a faithful minority to bring Gospel-centered reformation to the Church. I want to tell my grandchildren one day about how the Gospel cut through my time-bound prejudices—just as it did for abolitionists, suffragists, and civil rights marchers—and drove us, as followers of Jesus, to make a stand for biblical justice and equality. For the sake of the Gospel, I want you to be able to tell that story too.

Sources

[1] Roth, Cecil. *The Concise Jewish Encyclopedia*, New York City: New American Library, 1980, p. 424

[2] Cromartie, Michael. "Dr. Timothy Keller at the March 2013 Faith Angle Forum." *EPPC.org*. Ethics and Public Policy Center, 19 Mar. 2013. Web.

[3] Gallup Jr., Gordon. "Attitudes toward homosexuals and evolutionary theory: The role of evidence." *Ethology and Sociobiology*, Volume 17, Issue 4, July 1996, pp. 281-284

[4] Robinson, J. Armitage (translator), ed (1920). *Didache.* Barnabas, Hermar and the Didache. D.ii.2c. NY: The MacMillan Co.. pp. 112.

[5] Stark, Rodney; *The Rise of Christianity*, Princeton University Press, 1996, pp. 97-98

[6] Helminiak, Daniel A; *What the Bible Really Says About Homosexuality* (Millenium Edition), Alamo Square Press, April 2000. p. 23

[7] John Eastburn Boswell (American Council of Learned Societies); *Same-Sex Unions in Premodern Europe,* Random House, June 1994

[8] Callón, Callon. "Callón gaña o Vicente Risco de Ciencias Sociais cun ensaio sobre a homosexualidade na Idade Media" (in Galician) Galiciae.com, Web 27 February 2011.

[9] Goar, Jacques. "Euchologion Sive Rituale Graecorum Complectens Ritus Et Ordines Divinae Liturgiae." Venetiis: ex typographia Bartholomei Javarina, 1730. Hathitrust. [30], 735, [12] pp.

[10] Neill, James; *The Origins of and Role of Same-Sex Relations in Human Society*, McFarland and Company, Inc., 2009. p. 373

[11] Crompton, Louis; *Homosexuality and Civilization*, First Harvard University Press, 2006. pp. 186-187

[12] Malone, Mary; *Women in Christianity, Volume I*, Orbis Books, 2001. p. 125

[13] Kuefler, Mathew (2007). "The Marriage Revolution in Late Antiquity: The Theodosian Code and Later Roman Marriage Law." *Journal of Family History* 32 (4): 343–370. doi:10.1177/0363199007304424.

[14] Evagrius *Ecclesiastical History* 3.39

[15] Theodosian Code 9.7.6

[16] Clement of Alexandria, "The Instructor of Children" 2:10:91:2 [A.D. 191]

[17] Achtemeier, Mark. "Beers with Dr. Achtemeier." *Monk's Kaffe Pub*. Dubuque, Iowa. Aug. 2014

[18] Lewis, C. S. "Right and Wrong as a Clue to the Meaning of the Universe." In *Mere Christianity*, New York: MacMillan Pub, 1952.

[19] "Growing Support for Gay Marriage: Changed Minds and Changing Demographics." *Pew Research Center for the People and the Press RSS*. Pew Research Center, Web. 20 Mar. 2013.

[20] Gates, Gary J., and Frank Newport. "Special Report: 3.4% of U.S. Adults Identify as LGBT." *Gallup Politics*. Gallup, Web. 18 Oct. 2012.

[21] "Spiritual Profile of Homosexual Adults Provides Surprising Insights." *The Barna Group*, Web. 2009.

[22] "Survey Shows How the Faith of America's Hispanics Has Changed." *The Barna Group*, Web. 2009.

[23] Shilts, Randy; *And The Band Played on: Politics, People, and the AIDS Epidemic,* St. Martins Press, 1988. p. 347

[24] Patrologiae curses completus, Series Graeca, 88:1893-96

[25] Dallas, Joe. *A Strong Delusion: Confronting the "Gay Christian" Movement*: Harvest House, 1996. Web. Responding to Gay Theology Part III.

[26] MacArthur, John; *The MacArthur Bible Commentary,* Thomas Nelson Publishers, 2005, p. 1038.

[27] Plutarch, Moralia, 768E, Richard Elliott Friedman and Shawna Dolansky, *The Bible Now*, Oxford: Oxford University Press 2011, p. 34.

[28] Nissinen, *Homoeroticism in the Biblical World*, Augsburg Press, 1998, pp. 19-36.

[29] Plato, *Laws*, 840a, trans. K.J. Dover, *Greek Homosexuality;* Cambridge, MA: Harvard University Press, 1989, p. 65.

[30] Nissinen, *Homoeroticism in the Biblical World*, Augsburg Press, 1998, p. 19. Richard Elliott Friedman and Shawna Dolansky, *The Bible Now*, Oxford: Oxford University Press 2011, p 21-32. David F. Greenberg, *The Construction of Homosexuality*, Chicago: The University of Chicago Press, 1998, pp. 131-32, 135.

[31] Nissinen, *Homoeroticism in the Biblical World*, Augsburg Press, 1998, pp. 20-23.

[32] Philo of Alexandria, & Yonge, C. D. (1995). The works of Philo: Complete and unabridged (597–598 & 422–423). Peabody, MA: Hendrickson.

[33] English Standard Version (ESV), first published in 2001 by Crossway Bibles.

[34] Bretlinger, Rick. "Malachi Is Never Used in the Bible to Mean Homosexual." *Gay Christian 101*. 01 November 2011. Web.

[35] Martin, Dale B. "Arsenokoites and Malakos: Meanings and Consequences" *The Center of Gay and Lesbian Studies in Religion and Ministry*, Pacific School of Religion. Web. 1996

[36] Aristophanes, *Ecclesiazusae*, line 1058

[37] McRay, John; *Archaeology and the New Testament*, Baker Academic, 1991, pp. 315-316.

[38] Augustine, *City of God*, 6.7 (ed. R.W. Dyson, *The City of God Against the Pagans*; New York: Cambridge University Press, 1998), p. 254.

[39] Hippolytus, *Refutation of All Heresies*, Book V

[40] Robert, Gagnon A.J. " Bad Reasons for Changing One's Mind." *Dr. Robert A. J. Gagnon [Online].* N.p.,Web. 01 Mar. 2004.

[41] Formicas, *The Error of Pagan Religions*, 4.2

[42] *The Digest of Justinian, Vol. IV, University of Pennsylvania Press, Philadelphia, 1985, p. 944.*

[43] Cassius Dio, *Roman History*, LXII, 13

[44] Vines, Matthew, *The Gay Debate: The Bible and Homosexuality.* Youtube, 10 March, 2012. Web.

[45] Burroway, Jim. "First Look at Mark Regnerus's Study of Children of Parents in Same-Sex Relationships." *Box Turtle Bulletin.* 10 June 2012. Web.

[46] Gartrell, Nanette., Bos, Henny. "US National Longitudinal Lesbian Family Study: Psychological Adjustment of 17-Year-Old Adolescents." *Pediatrics.* 07 June 2010.

[47] Simon R Crouch, Elizabeth Waters, Ruth McNair, Jennifer Power, Elise Davis. "Parent-reported measures of child health and wellbeing in same-sex parent families: a cross-sectional survey." *BMC Public Health*. 21 June 2014.

[48] Driscoll, Mark/Grace; *Real Marriage: The Truth About Sex, Friendship, and Life Together,* Thomas Nelson, 2012, p. 188.

[49] Hill, Wesley. "Homosexuality and Impatience for Joy." First Things. 23 March, 2013. Web.

[50] Calabia, Alison. "Teens and Sex." *Psychology Today*. N.p., 01 July 2001. Web.

[51] Hooker, E. (1957). "The Adjustment of the Male Overt Homosexual." *Journal of Projective Techniques, 21,* pp. 18-31.

[52] Gottman, J. M., Levenson, R. W., Swanson, C., Swanson, K., Tyson, R., & Yoshimoto, D. (2003). "Observing gay, lesbian and heterosexual couples' relationships: mathematical modeling of conflict interaction." Journal of Homosexuality, 45(1), 65-91.

[53] Gottman, John M. "Correlates of Gay and Lesbian Couples' Relationship Satisfaction and Relationship Dissolution" Journal of Homosexuality, Vol. 45(1) 2003. Web.

[54] Meyer, Ilan H. "Prejudice, Social Stress, and Mental Health in Lesbian, Gay, and Bisexual Populations: Conceptual Issues and Research Evidence." *Psychological Bulletin* 129.5 (2003): 674-97. Print.

[55] "America's Most and Least Bible-Minded Cities." *Barna: Cities*. Barna Group, May 2012. Web.

[56] Achtemeier, Mark. "And Grace Will Lead Me Home: Inclusion and Evangelical Conscience." *Address delivered to the Covenant Network of Presbyterians*, Covenant Network, 30 November, 2009. Web.

[57] "Insufficient Evidence That Sexual Orientation Change Efforts Work." *APA*. American Psychological Association, 5 Aug. 2009. Web.

[58] American Medical Association: Policy Statement H-160.991, "Health Care Needs of the Homosexual Population."

[59] Benedict, Carey. "Psychiatry Giant Sorry for Backing Gay 'Cure'." *The New York Times.* 18 May 2012, Health sec. Print.

[60] Eckholm, Erik. "Rift Forms in Movement as Belief in Gay 'Cure' Is Renounced." *The New York Times* 6 July 2012, U.S. sec. Print.

[61] Steffan, Melissa. "Former Ex-Gay Spokesman John Paul Apologizes Amid Divorce." *Gleanings*. Christianity Today, 2 May 2013. Web.

[62] Taylor, Justin. "Homosexuality & the Christian Faith: A Lecture by and Q&A with Rosaria Butterfield." *Between Two Worlds*. The Gospel Coalition, 15 July 2013. Web.

[63] Butterfield, Rosaria. "My Train Wreck Conversion." *Testimony*. Christianity Today, 7 September 2013. Web.

[64] Eternity News. "New Website Created by Three Anglican Ministers Who Experience Same-Sex Attraction." *News*. Bible Society, 5 December 2013. Web. www.livingout.org

[65] Hill, Wesley. "Same-Sex Attraction and Spiritual Friendship Q&A," Address at Saint Johns Parish. 12, December, 2014. Web. www.st-johns.squarespace.com/sermons

[66] Knapp, Jennifer. "Same-Sex Marriage: The Love That Dares Speak Its Name." *Huffpost Gay Voices*. The Huffington Post, 10 May 2012. Web.

[67] *New Englander and Yale review*, Volume 43, Issue 179 (March 1884), pp. 193-213.

[68] Thornwell, James. *The Collected Writings of James Thornwell, Volume 4*, Richmond Presbyterian Committee of Publication, 1873, p 385

[69] Charleston Union Presbytery, *New York Evangelist*, November 21, 1835, p 258.

[70] Jones, Jeffrey M. "Same-Sex Marriage Support Solidifies Above 50% in U.S." *Gallop Politics*. Gallup, 13 May 2013. Web.

[71] Lewis, C. S. "Right and Wrong as a Clue to the Meaning of the Universe." In *Mere Christianity*, New York: MacMillan Pub, 1952.

[72] "Seven in 10 Young Adults Favor Same-Sex Marriage." *Pew Research Center Daily Number*. Pew Research Center, 6 May 2013. Web.

[73] "Fact Sheet Gay and Lesbian Issues." *Public Religion*. Public Religion Research Institute, 4 Apr. 2013. Web.

[74] William, James. "The Will to Believe." First published in *The New World*, Volume 5 (1896): pp. 327-347

[75] Wunderink, Susan. "What to Do about Unbiblical Unions." *Christianity Today*. June 2009, Feature.

[76] Smith Sr., James A. "Pro-gay book 'exceedingly dangerous'" *Baptist Press*. 22 Apr. 2014. Web. Quoting Albert Mohler, President of the Southern Baptist Theological Seminary, pro-LGBT evangelical theology, "Could be for some of those wavering evangelicals the kind of off-ramp for which they've been searching. However, it is a fatally flawed argument. And it will take them into a non-evangelical identity."

Contact

If you would like to contact the author, you can reach him at ToMeltAGoldenCalf@gmail.com.

Printed in Great Britain
by Amazon